LIFE AND DEATH IN LONDON'S EAST END

2000 years at Spitalfields

LIFE AND DEATH IN LONDON'S EAST END

2000 years at Spitalfields

CHRIS THOMAS

MUSEUM OF LONDON
Archaeology Service

Spitalfields Development Group
A subsidiary of Hammerson plc

Hammerson

CORPORATION OF LONDON

Published in April 2004 by the
Museum of London Archaeology Service

A CIP catalogue record for this book is available from
the British Library

ISBN 1 901992 49 7

The following institutions and individuals are thanked
for their permission to reproduce illustrations on the
pages indicated
Ashmolean Museum, Oxford 32; La Biblioteca
Medicea 42; The British Library 44, 45, 54, 56, 57,
60; Codrington Library, All Souls College, University
of Oxford 94; English Heritage 73; Foster and
Partners 9; Peter Froste 17; Nigel Hillyard 75;
Guildhall Library, Corporation of London 53, 66, 68,
71, 80, 81, 89, 95; Hospices de Beaunes 42; Derek
Lucas 14; London Metropolitan Archive 86, 88, 89,
91, 98; The National Gallery, London 40; Royal
Library of Belgium, Brussels 47; Spitalfields
Development Group 2; Stedelijke Musea Brugge 43;
John Sturrock 3, 9, 11, 97; Julian Thurgood 38, 40;
Warburg Institute 94; The Whitworth Art Gallery, The
University of Manchester 92

CONTENTS

Foreword   2

Acknowledgements   3

Introduction   7

The Roman cemetery   15

The medieval priory and hospital of St Mary Spital   31

The Artillery Ground   67

From aristocratic enclave to suburb of immigrants   77

The redevelopment of Spitalfields   87

Further reading   99

Glossary   100

FOREWORD

The excavations at Spitalfields were the most impressive that I have worked on, not simply because of their sheer scale but because of the dedication and professionalism of everyone on site, from the director to the 'diggers'. It would have been very easy for the thousands of human burials to be regarded simply as numbers – piles of bones to be got out of the ground as quickly as possible. But no one that worked at Spitalfields seemed to lose sight of the fact that these were the remains of people, of our ancestors, and that each had a story to tell.

For me as an archaeologist Spitalfields brought me face to face with the complexities and challenges of over 30 burials in one grave, not an experience that I feel I would enjoy on a regular basis. And for me as a programme maker, what came out of this site were the fascinating stories of two contrasting individuals – the Roman 'princess' and the medieval 'pauper'. Soon their stories will join with those that will emerge from the painstaking analysis of all of the burials, helping to create a unique window on life and death in historic London. Spitalfields is an excavation to be justifiably proud of.

JULIAN RICHARDS

LEFT Spitalfields in the foreground with the City behind, taken prior to redevelopment (courtesy of the Spitalfields Development Group)

ACKNOWLEDGEMENTS

The new residential development on the left along Folgate Street, designed to fit in with the neighbouring Georgian terraces (John Sturrock)

This book is the result of the dedication, hard work and skill of an enormous number of people: archaeologists, surveyors, find specialists, environmental specialists and many others. The Spitalfields Project has been funded by a large number of organisations but principal amongst these has been the Spitalfields Development Group, who have been the driving force behind the redevelopment of the area; our thanks in particular go to the chief executive, Mike Bear, and to Steve Wood and Toby Brown. Other important backers of the archaeological projects have been St George PLC; the ABN Amro Bank; Hammerson PLC; the Corporation of London; Mercury Asset Management Ltd; Scottish Life Assurance Co; Ballymore Properties Ltd; and the London International Finance, Futures and Options Exchange. The project managers for the project were Second London Wall Project Management Ltd and thanks in particular go to Mike Blinco, Lee Sims, Shane Lincoln and Max Highfield. We would also like to thank all the engineers and architects, who have been of immense help: Tony Taylor and colleagues of Foggo Associates; Rob Kinch and colleagues of Arups; and John Drew and colleagues of Foster and Partners.

The work on site could also never have been accomplished without the help of numerous contractors, in particular: Tony Hewitt, Mick Mills, Adrian Rogers and Mike Hand of Balfour Beatty; John Stroker, Bobby Ellis and Martyn Drake of Keltbray; Mick, Dennis, John and Albert of L and B; and Graham Lill of McAlpine.

The help and support of English Heritage has been central to the success of the project and we would especially like to thank Ellen

Barnes, Nick Truckle, Jane Sidell, Steven Brindle, Charmian Baker, Simon Mays and Alex Bayliss. Thanks should also go to the all those others who have willingly given their views on or supported the excavation of this site, in particular Barney Sloane.

Finally, this book is the combination of the work of numerous people, mostly from MoLAS, who have worked on the project and made it such a success. The site supervisors were Rosalind Aitken, David Bowsher, Mark Burch, Jessica Cowley, Andy Daykin, Lesley Dunwoodie, Chiz Harward, Nick Holder, Isca Howell, Malcolm McKenzie, Adrian Miles, Ken Pitt, Paul Thrale and Lucy Thompson. The project managers were the author and Paul Falcini. The osteologists were Brian Connell, Amy Grey-Jones, Natasha Powers, Rebecca Redfern, Don Walker and Bill White. Research on the finds has been carried out by Liz Barham, Geoff Egan, Rupert Featherby, Nigel Jeffries, Lyn Keys, Jackie Keily, Alison Nailer, Mark Samuel, Terry Smith and Roy Stephenson; research on the environmental evidence was by Jane Corcoran, Lisa Grey-Rees and Jane Liddle. Numerous other people made a substantial contribution to the success of the Spitalfields Project and in particular to the visitor centre that was opened on site; many of these people were volunteers and staffed it in their own time and particular thanks go to Rosemary Yeaxlee and Laura Schaaf. The visitor centre itself was designed by Andy Chopping and constructed by Andy Chopping, Steve Tompkins, Jeanette van der Post, Edwin Baker, Maggie Cox, Andy Murray and Cliff Thomas. The photographs in this book, except where otherwise stated, are by Andy Chopping, Maggie Cox and Edwin Baker. The plans are by Peter Hart-Allison and Ken Lymer and the principal reconstructions are by Faith Vardy. The text was edited by Sue Hirst, Sue Wright and Peter Rowsome. The book was designed, typeset and produced by Tracy Wellman.

Thanks are due to all the hundreds of people who worked on the project both on and off site: without them this book would never have been possible.

LEFT Commercial Street in 1907 with Spitalfields Market on the left

RIGHT The archaeological team in 1999 – well over 100 people were working on site in the summer of that year

INTRODUCTION

Spitalfields is one of London's most culturally diverse and historic areas. It has been, throughout history, on the margins – a stone's throw from the mercantile centre and yet often impoverished and overlooked. It has been a focus for migrants and immigrants for over 800 years, and the mix of these people has made it one of the most exciting and surprising districts within the capital. This book tells the story of the area over the last 2000 years.

In 1987 the London Borough of Tower Hamlets and the Corporation of London decided to move the fruit and vegetable market at Spitalfields out of central London, in line with the removal of other London markets like Covent Garden and Billingsgate. This would drastically reduce the congestion on the local streets and the noise of trading throughout the early hours of the morning. A new Spitalfields Market was built and opened in 1991, on the east side of the River Lea in Leyton, and

so over 300 years of a working market in Spitalfields came to an end. This meant that traders had to move and caused a major change in the way of life of many local people.

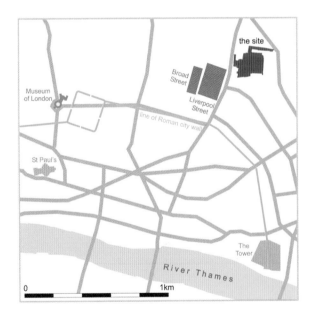

The site under excavation in 1999; in the background is Christ Church which still dominates the area

Moving the market created an opportunity to redevelop and regenerate a large area right next to the City of London; one that had traditionally been very poor. The 19th-century market buildings, which were listed, were retained, whilst plans were drawn up to demolish the 1920s and 1930s buildings, and to redevelop the area for offices, shops and housing.

Archaeologists had been working in Spitalfields, from time to time, since the 1930s and had demonstrated the archaeological importance of the area. It had been used as a burial ground by the Romans, was the site of one of the country's most important and largest medieval hospitals, and was the site of one of London's earliest suburbs. As a result much of it was made a Scheduled Ancient

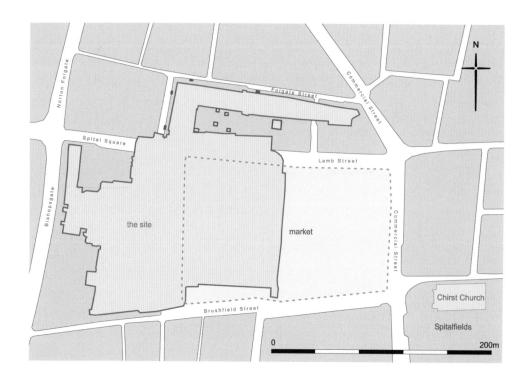

ABOVE LEFT Demolishing the 1928 extension to Spitalfields Market created thousands of tonnes of concrete and steel

LEFT A plan with the excavated areas coloured in pink showing the enormous scale of the project

CLOCKWISE FROM TOP LEFT
An architect's impression
of the new building on
Bishop Square (Foster
and Partners); 250
Bishopsgate – the new
headquarters of the

ABN Amro Bank (John
Sturrock); an architect's
impression of the
viewing gallery for the
preserved medieval
charnel house (Foster
and Partners)

Monument in 1987, which meant that the archaeology was protected by law and that the ground could not be disturbed without agreement with the government and consideration for its archaeological value.

The large size of the site – 5.2 hectares or almost 13 acres – was unparalleled as an archaeological investigation in an urban centre. The original layers beneath some of the market buildings had been destroyed by their basements but much of the site lay over roads and car parks, where there was a complete record of the history of the area from the 1930s back to the Roman period – almost 2000 years of undisturbed history, waiting to be rediscovered. Some of the site was preserved but in the end some 3.25 hectares were excavated containing more than 80,000m³ of archaeological deposits.

ARCHAEOLOGY

Archaeological excavation is essentially a destructive process, removing the layers of soil, buildings and finds in a never-to-be-repeated experiment. Thus current policy is not to dig up sites but, wherever possible, to preserve them *in situ* for future generations. Of course this is not always possible and in Spitalfields it was felt that the need for redevelopment and regeneration, and the needs of both the local and national economy outweighed the importance of preserving the archaeological deposits. It was also a fundamental principle of the new development that the traffic should be confined to below ground level, leaving the ground level as a series of courtyards, squares and passages for pedestrian use. This required a very large basement with a vehicular access ramp, destroying all the archaeological remains on the site.

Certain provisions were made to ensure preservation of part of the monument: for instance, the ramp was moved to preserve the walls of the medieval church. These parts were exposed, protected and then reburied. Also, a remarkable find of a charnel house – a medieval building for storing human bones – was made and the developers generously agreed to keep this building. After much work by archaeologists, engineers and architects, this will now have its own dedicated basement, accessible to all, with the building serving as a reminder of the site's past.

A massive programme of archaeological excavation was set in place which ran, on and off, for 12 years, funded by the developers: government policy requires that the developers of a site who are destroying its archaeological remains should pay for archaeologists to excavate and record them.

Wrapping up the charnel house in 1999 to protect the walls from damage by frost

The glass divide

When the proposals for the redevelopment of Spitalfields were first made, they engendered much opposition. Many local people were opposed to the redevelopment as it would change their locality and community. Mike Bear, the chief executive of the Spitalfields Development Group, used to describe Bishopsgate as a 'glass wall' – an artificial barrier between the office-based City and the residential-based Spitalfields.

A planning inquiry and the property crash of the early 1990s prevented development, and the Spitalfields Development Group needed a way of utilising the site now that the fruit and vegetable market had been relocated. They decided to make use of the site with a number of initiatives: car parking; a swimming pool; space for local artists' studios; sports pitches;

and, most importantly, a local market. Ironically, the success of these enterprises proved a severe handicap to the progress of the development – many local people wanted to keep these new amenities even though they had only been temporary measures.

The new flats and the new offices along Bishopsgate proved not to be too contentious but many locals were strongly opposed to the demolition of the 1928 extension to Spitalfields Market. After a protracted struggle, the appointment of the architects Foster and Partners and the retention of part of the market along the view line to Christchurch finally convinced enough people to support the demolition of most of the market and the erection of new offices. The Victorian market buildings, which are listed, still stand and the market thrives, but many local people will need to be convinced that encroachment of office space into their local community will not adversely affect it in the long term.

BELOW The 1928 extension to Spitalfields Market; construction of this building destroyed much of the archaeology and removed more than 1000 skeletons without record

BELOW RIGHT Elder Gardens and the new residential development (John Sturrock)

INVOLVING THE PUBLIC

Working on such a large site gave us an opportunity to involve the general public – a fundamental part of the Museum of London's work. It was also important to show the commitment of the developers to the archaeology and history of the site, particularly considering the opposition to the idea of development. Archaeology was just one of many initiatives that the Spitalfields Development Group sponsored to demonstrate their commitment to the local community.

We displayed posters around Spitalfields Market, which were regularly updated with new discoveries, and took local groups, school parties and archaeological societies around the site. We also created a website and built our own visitor centre in the Market, which, opening at lunchtimes and on Sundays, attracted over 27,000 people in the Summer of 1999. It contained information and artefacts from the site, and overlooked the site so that the public could see the archaeologists working.

We were also inundated by TV companies wanting to film on the site – two programmes were made by BBC's Meet the Ancestors team and another by London News Network. Television companies from around the world filmed at the site: from Italy, New Zealand, and USA, to take just a few examples.

Long-term public involvement was fostered by creating displays in the new buildings and making the medieval charnel house a site that can be visited.

THE ROMAN CEMETERY

Early Roman London

Londinium was founded shortly after the Roman invasion of AD 43 and in its early years probably looked much like an American frontier town with small shops and houses built out of earth and timber built along the roads around the middle of the city and close to the docks. The Boudican rebellion and fire of AD 60 and a later fire during the reign of the Emperor Hadrian in the 120s destroyed much of the town, requiring major rebuilding programmes. At this time, Spitalfields lay just beyond the city boundaries and its natural soil, known as brickearth, was extensively quarried to make floors and walls and for making bricks and tiles. We can imagine that plots of land were handed over to gangs who systematically dug out the brickearth and brought it back into the town on carts along the adjacent road. At the same time people were digging wells in the area which they lined with timber. When one of these went out of use, a group of pots was thrown down it; perhaps this was an offering to the earth deity in compensation for the digging of the well.

The focus of the town was trade and so some of its most important and well-built structures lay along the river. The Romans built massive river walls from timber with quays and wharves along the Thames, where the bustling Roman dockers could load and unload ships, and the wealthy merchants could store their goods. Away from the docks, on the road leading from London Bridge, lay the forum – the hub of any Roman city – where much of daily Roman life was carried out. The town included public baths, an amphitheatre, temples and many of the other buildings usually associated with Roman culture. All were linked by the efficient road system for which the Romans were famous. These roads were made of gravel, which was also quarried in Spitalfields and other areas around the town.

LEFT A reconstruction of a Roman burial scene (Derek Lucas)

RIGHT Roman pots thrown down a well in about AD 120

London in the later Roman period

The character of London was very different in the 3rd and 4th centuries AD. The frontier town, full to overflowing with craftsmen and traders, became a town with fewer but often wealthier people: in the 2nd century the population may have been about 20,000 and this fell to perhaps 10,000 in the 4th century. By the 3rd century, high stone walls and gates enclosed the city on three sides, and a wall was also eventually built along the riverfront. These structures were both a demonstration of London's status and importance, and a defence against marauding raiders. The wall along the river also blocked the easy access to the river; and must have signalled a slowdown in the importing and exporting of goods from the docks.

LEFT A recreation of a 4th-century Roman Londoner's dining room
BELOW LEFT A comb and manicure set – the set consists of five implements for personal hygiene including tweezers, a nail file and a scoop for cosmetics
BELOW A reconstruction of the late Roman town where the modern road of Poultry met the line of the River Walbrook, reduced at this date to a small stream (Judith Dobie)

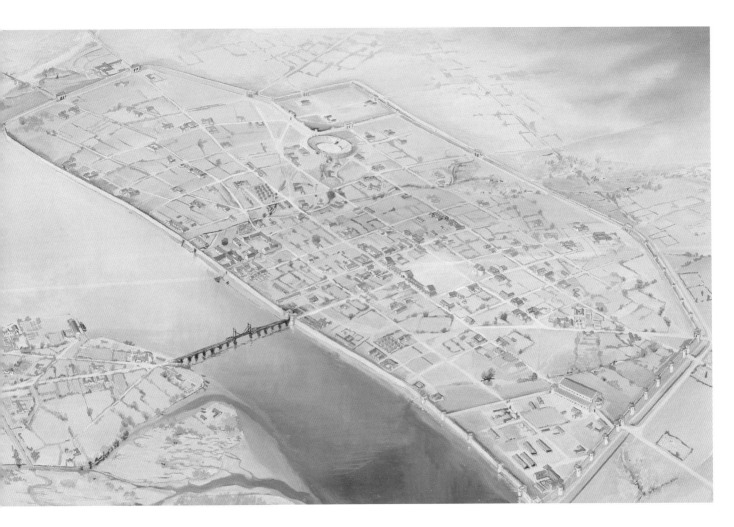

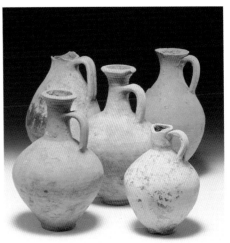

ABOVE A reconstruction of late Roman London – the crowded streets lined with small houses have been replaced by fewer, larger properties signifying the smaller but wealthier population (Peter Froste)

RIGHT Five of the pots from the Roman well at Spitalfields

Many of the larger houses in later Roman London were built of stone, with fine mosaic floors, instead of the old earth and timber houses. Some even had their own bathhouses, replacing the public baths that had gone out of use. Many of these people were likely to have been wealthy merchants or important government officials. The wealthiest are likely to have had country estates as well as their London town house. They lived in a style and opulence far removed from the living conditions of their predecessors only a hundred years earlier.

The Spitalfields cemetery

Roman law forbade burial within the town limits, so the Romans usually buried their dead alongside the roads out of town. In London there were cemeteries to the south along the roads out of Southwark; to the east of Londinium in the Aldgate area; to the west along what is now Newgate; and to the north along the line of Bishopsgate – originally called Ermine Street – where modern Spitalfields lies, about 400m outside of Londinium. Archaeologists have recovered well over 1500 Roman burials from London's cemeteries.

LEFT A Roman skeleton lying on a bed of chalk, a common burial practice BELOW Reconstruction of the burial of the woman in the lead coffin – the lead coffin was lowered into the stone sarcophagus in the grave and the glass phial placed beside it before the lids of the lead coffin and the stone sarcophagus were put in place (Faith Vardy)

The first record of burials being found at Spitalfields, to the east of Ermine Street, dates to the end of the 16th century, when John Stow wrote in his Survey of London:

On the east side of this churchyard lieth a large field, of old time called Lolesworth now Spittle field; which about the year 1576 was broken up for clay to make brick; in the digging whereof many earthen pots, called urnae, were found full of ashes, and burnt bones of men, to wit, of the Romans that inhabited here

and again:

There hath also been found in the same field divers coffins of stone, containing the bones of men.... Moreover, there were also found the skulls and bones of men without coffins, or rather whose coffins (being of great timber) were consumed.

Many Romans were buried with grave goods: either something to accompany them on their journey to the afterlife; a part of the burial ritual; or personal effects of sentimental value. Roman cemeteries can be very difficult to date, as some grave goods may be heirlooms, but the cemetery at Spitalfields seems mostly to date to the later Roman period, approximately AD 250–400. So, many of the dead found buried in Spitalfields probably relate to that later period of Roman London, when it was inhabited by fewer but often wealthier people. Given the opulence of some of the graves, it seems that some of these people were indeed buried at Spitalfields.

CLOCKWISE FROM ABOVE
A Roman burial laid in chalk and surrounded by five pots; the five pots – four beakers and a dish – laid around the Roman skeleton; a Roman buried without grave goods – about 75% of the Roman burials did not have artefacts accompanying them

DISCOVERY

In March 1999, we made one of the most extraordinary discoveries from London in the recent past – a stone sarcophagus or coffin lay at the southern edge of the cemetery plot. The last one of these to be found in London was discovered in the early 1970s, so we knew we had a rare and unusual find. The Meet the Ancestors TV team came to film us excavating it. The first task was to excavate the grave surrounding the sarcophagus; there we found a jet hairpin and small box, and a unique glass phial with an accompanying jet 'stick'.

When we finally removed the lid of the sarcophagus we found a complete decorated lead coffin inside. Whilst we have found lead coffins in Roman cemeteries on occasion in the past, the combination of stone sarcophagus and lead coffin was very rare: the last such to be found in London was in 1876 and none had been dug up by archaeologists.

BELOW FROM LEFT
Examining the stone sarcophagus before removing its lid; jet and glass artefacts buried within the grave but outside the sarcophagus; removal of the sarcophagus lid revealed an intact lead coffin within; preparing the sarcophagus for

This made our find even more important and we had to decide how best to excavate it. If the lead coffin were sealed, or even reasonably airtight, then very rare materials might survive which might be difficult to excavate and preserve on site; and, if it were airtight, there might be a health risk to the public if the body had only partially decomposed.

We decided to lift the sarcophagus and transport it to the Museum of London where it could be excavated in safety and with all the required scientific equipment on hand. We built a cradle of steel girders around the sarcophagus and prepared to transfer it to a waiting lorry, in front of the world's media. It was so heavy that it had to be lifted by a machine that had to track across site, drive it up a ramp and lower it onto the lorry. We were concerned that anything inside would get damaged during this process. But we need not have worried – our machine driver was so good that there were no mishaps.

transportation whilst being filmed by the BBC's Meet the Ancestors team; unloading the sarcophagus at the Museum of London where it was to be excavated; removing the lead coffin from the sarcophagus at the Museum of London's archive at Eagle Wharf Road

Days later, after conservators had cleaned the coffin lid to reveal its beautiful scallop-shell decoration, the time came to open the lead coffin, once again in front of the press. As we removed the lid, we saw beneath it the well-preserved skeleton of a woman lying in wet silt. The remains of leaves, textiles and other organic material surviving in the silt confirmed our decision to excavate the coffin in the Museum of London as the correct one. Fortunately there were no attendant health risks, as the coffin was not airtight.

After photographing and recording the position of the bones, we lifted them and took them to the conservation laboratory, where we carefully washed them.

BELOW FROM LEFT The team examining the sarcophagus immediately after removal of the lid of the lead coffin – the suits and masks were worn to prevent contamination of any DNA samples from the skeleton and to protect the team from the effects of any lead dust from the coffin; conservators cleaning the lid of the lead coffin reveal its remarkable scallop-shell decoration; thousands of visitors poured into the Museum of London to see the 'princess' in the sarcophagus, as she became known, and to watch the conservators excavating the coffin and revealing its remarkable secrets

LEFT Archaeologists and conservators examining the bones of the woman in the sarcophagus

BELOW Headline news

© The Evening Standard

© The Sunday Express

© The Eastern Daily Press

Face of fourth century is unveiled

SCIENTISTS RECREATE THE FACE OF LONDON'S 1,700-YEAR-OLD 'TARA'

The Roman It girl

Museum lifts the lid on a First Lady of London

by PETER GRUNER

The following morning the bones were laid out on display and, after a press conference, conservators began the painstaking excavation of the coffin in front of the public. By 10am the queues ran all the way through the Museum and out of the front door. In the next three days over 10,000 people came to the Museum of London to see the work going on; many thousands more came over the following days and weeks. Many described it as an unforgettable experience, particularly if they were there when one of the other remarkable finds – such as the second glass phial – was seen for the first time in over 1600 years.

The sarcophagi

The wealthiest members of Roman society wanted a burial and a monument that befitted their status. In one area of the cemetery we found just such a high status burial plot. A row of four graves once held stone sarcophagi, although only the one described in the previous section survived later grave robbers. Only fragments of the other sarcophagi survived, thrown back into the graves after the robbers had made off with what they wanted.

The surviving sarcophagus was made from Barnack stone, imported from the East Midlands. Mining, carving and importing such a coffin would have taken a long time, so it is likely that the family must either have already owned it or they must have bought it from a coffin seller somewhere in Londinium. The lead for the lead coffin was probably mined from the Mendip Hills in Somerset. The scallop shell decoration on its lid is a common motif on Roman lead coffins. It may be a reference to the soul's final journey across the Ocean to the Isles of the Blessed and came to symbolise rebirth and fertility in Romano-Celtic religion.

FAR LEFT The sarcophagus of the 'princess', lead coffin, skeleton and artefacts on display at the Museum of London
BELOW A drawing of scallop-shell decoration on a lead coffin lid from a nearby site
BELOW BOTTOM The smashed fragments of another sarcophagus found only a few metres from the preserved one

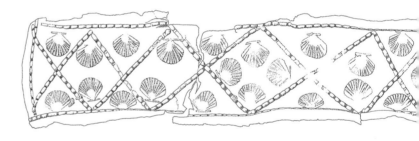

Inside the coffin lay the skeleton of a young woman of about 25 years of age. We do not know what she died of, as there were no obvious signs of disease on her skeleton, but we know she had not had children. Her head was laid on a pillow of bay leaves; fragments of wool suggested that there was once a pillowcase around them. There were also fragments of other textiles on her skeleton, which suggest what she may have been wearing when she was buried. Silk damask, an expensive cloth, was perhaps used in the main item of clothing. Fragments of 22 carat gold thread – only the third such find in the UK – were mostly found around her neck and thighs, suggesting she may have worn a short tunic of silk, edged in gold thread. DNA analysis and oxygen isotope analysis were carried out on her teeth, leading to some remarkable conclusions. Both suggested she was originally from southern Europe and not the UK; the closest match from the DNA was from someone from the Basque region of Spain. Perhaps she was from a high-ranking wealthy family, her father an important official who had been sent to London on business from somewhere around the Mediterranean.

The decoration on the unique glass phial has, however, been seen before on other artefacts and it is that which gives us a clue to when this woman was buried – right at the end of the Roman period in London – between AD 350 and AD 410.

Bay leaves preserved within the lead coffin; these had formed part of a pillow beneath the woman's head and had been preserved by the coffin lead

The remarkable finds from the sarcophagus – the glass phial is a unique piece but the decoration is known from other artefacts and tells us that the phial was made after AD 350; next to it are fragments of a jet box (which has now been reconstructed but is very fragile); the three other objects are all also made of jet and comprise accessories for tying up her hair and a rod for dipping into the glass phial, presumably when it held some form of fragrant liquid

DNA & ISOTOPE ANALYSIS

New techniques constantly become available to archaeologists. Two that we used at Spitalfields were DNA and isotope analysis: both can help us to understand the origins of people.

We decided to try to extract samples of DNA from some of the Roman skeletons, particularly the woman from the sarcophagus, to see if we could find out where they had come from and if any of these people were related. Amazingly DNA still survived in the teeth of these skeletons (although not in the bone) and scientists were able to tell that the skeletons that were tested were not related by blood. Unfortunately, not many other archaeologists have tested for DNA, so we do not have many people to compare but we were able to tell that the closest match for our woman in the sarcophagus from a modern database of 10,000 Europeans was to someone from the Basque region of Spain.

We also extracted samples from the same tooth for oxygen, nitrogen and lead isotope analysis. The most interesting of these was the oxygen isotope analysis. The basic principle of oxygen isotope analysis is that oxygen is made up of atoms with slightly different chemical make-ups. Water from different parts of the world contains different proportions of these isotopes and, when we drink that water, we take tiny traces of that into our teeth. But this only occurs after we have lost our milk teeth and before our adult teeth become covered in enamel. This means that if you take a sample of someone's teeth and measure the isotopes you can tell where that person was drinking water when they were aged about seven. The results suggested that our woman in the sarcophagus had been living in southern Europe at that time, which fitted well with the DNA evidence that she may have come from Spain.

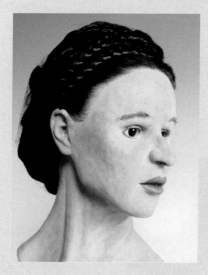

LEFT The reconstructed head of the woman from the sarcophagus
ABOVE Images of the head taken during the reconstruction process

The underground burial chamber

Although the other stone sarcophagi had been robbed out, fragments of a lid were found in another important grave right next to the surviving sarcophagus. This grave was an underground burial chamber, for the burial of at least two people. The person in the sarcophagus had been removed but the skeleton of a young child aged between 7 and 12, buried in a layer of chalk-like material, still remained. We cannot tell the sex of the child but DNA analysis tells us that the child was not related to the woman in the complete sarcophagus next to the mausoleum. The underground chamber itself was a timber structure, only the base of which survived. It would originally have had posts at the corners and planks along its sides.

The child was buried with an extraordinary array of beautiful glass vessels. These broke when the chamber collapsed and the earth fell in, many centuries ago, but a conservator has painstakingly reconstructed them. Four were large flasks and two were small beakers, which had fallen on the legs of the child. There was also a shallow bowl and fragments of a beaker with letters on, although not enough survives for us to read the text.

These glass vessels form one of the finest collections of glass buried in a single grave in south-east England. The people buried in this structure were again very wealthy and important members of society. The vessels certainly date to the late Roman period (ie the 4th century) and the chamber was probably constructed at a similar time to the burial of the sarcophagus with the lead coffin.

No grave goods survive from the other sarcophagi but we can see that this was an area of burial for some of the highest-ranking members of Roman society in London. If we remember Stow's words, it is clear that there were once many more such burials in the Spitalfields area.

The other Roman burials

We found about 150 Roman graves across the Spitalfields site, although people had destroyed many more in the medieval period whilst they were digging graves and pits. The preservation of the skeletons varied hugely; in one example of two graves side-by-side, one contained a complete skeleton and the other nothing but the feet inside a pair of hobnail boots.

A few people were cremated: some placed in pots; one in a specially designed glass cremation urn; and others simply buried in small pits.

About a quarter of all the people buried were accompanied by grave goods of some kind. One group of people were buried with small unguentariae – small jars shaped like miniature amphorae or wine jars – thought to have been

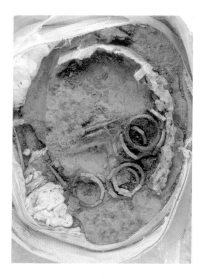

CLOCKWISE FROM TOP LEFT

A Roman skeleton laid on a layer of chalk (a sewer pipe from underground toilets built in the 1920s has cut the skeleton in half); one of many small 'unguentariae' – pottery vessels – buried with a group of individuals; a small 'motto' pot made in Trier in the late Roman period; bracelets, pins and beads in a wooden box with metal fittings, found with the skeleton of a child; some of the finds from the box after conservation

RIGHT A group of burials, perhaps a family, most of whom were buried with unguentariae

BELOW RIGHT Excavating another glass phial, this time buried at the feet; these vessels are rare and only seem to be found with burials – we now have four from Spitalfields

BELOW The complete glass phial found between the stone sarcophagus and the lead coffin

used for holding unguents. This group may have been a family and in one corner of the grave was a small niche containing a baby. Two other people were also buried with glass phials like those found with the sarcophagus; these are exceptionally unusual and may have played a part in the burial ceremony. One young person was buried with a collection of artefacts that may have been personal possessions. We do not know what sex the child was but the artefacts suggest she was a young girl. She was buried with a small beaker made in Trier, in south-west Germany, a small glass flask and a decayed circular wooden box with metal strips and handles. Inside the box was a line of beads that had originally been on a necklace and a group of shale bracelets – perhaps items of her personal jewellery. One person was buried with a pot containing a chicken – perhaps something to sustain them on their journey into the afterlife.

THE MEDIEVAL PRIORY AND HOSPITAL OF ST MARY SPITAL

THE MEDIEVAL PRIORY AND HOSPITAL OF ST MARY SPITAL

London in the 12th century

After the collapse of Roman rule in the early 5th century, Londinium was abandoned. In the 7th century the newly named trading centre of Lundenwic was built where Covent Garden now lies, to the west of a religious and possible administrative centre inside the old Roman city. Lundenwic, in turn, was abandoned at the end of the 9th century when the old walled city was re-inhabited, probably to afford the population some protection from Viking raids. This new town, known as Lundenburh, grew rapidly, with expanding trade and markets increasing the wealth of its merchants. By the end of the 1100s London had its own lord mayor and government, in the form of sheriffs and aldermen who administered the City. This increased wealth and trade meant more and more people were working and living in London.

London was surrounded on three sides by its stone walls with a ditch beyond and by the Thames on the fourth; the River Fleet lay to the west of the city walls. The medieval cathedral of St Paul dominated the city on the west side with the harbour and port ranged along the Thames frontage. The two main areas of port were at Queenhithe and Billingsgate. Between them lay London Bridge, re-established for the first time since the Roman period in the late 9th century and rebuilt in stone in the late 12th century, when it was lined with shops and houses. The bridge linked the suburb of Southwark across the river with the City.

Beyond the city, leading out of the main gates, were roads surrounded by fields. As the population grew, people built houses alongside these roads, creating new suburbs, which eventually joined up with the surrounding villages.

A reconstruction of St Mary Spital from the southeast in about 1500 – the pulpit and charnel house are in the cemetery in the foreground with the church and infirmaries behind (Faith Vardy)

The founding of St Mary Spital

The growing population gave rise to a need for hospitals to look after the sick, the poor and pilgrims. The earliest hospitals in London were for lepers, out in the open fields to the west of the city. These were at St Giles's where the 18th-century church now stands and at St James's, roughly on the site of St James's Palace. The first hospital for the general population was founded at St Bartholomew's in 1123 and soon there were others: St Thomas of Acon in the City, St Katherine near the Tower of London and St Thomas in Southwark. The Hospital of St Mary-without-Bishopsgate was founded in this wave of enthusiasm for charitable gifts, allegedly in about 1197. The hospital was soon known as St Mary Spital (spital being a shortening of the word hospital).

ABOVE LEFT A 12th-century pot being excavated

LEFT Wyngaerde's panorama of London of about 1540, showing St Mary Spital at the back (Ashmolean Museum, Oxford)

ABOVE A section through
the 12th-century water
supply alongside
Bishopsgate

ABOVE RIGHT View of
Greyfriars, established in
1225, at Newgate; the
early 13th century saw
the establishment of
many of London's
religious houses (Judith
Dobie)

The fields outside the hospital were known as Lolesworth Fields but soon became known as Spital Fields and hence the name of the district today. Like most of the other hospitals, St Mary Spital was built just outside of the city walls, as there was more available land in those areas and incoming migrants and pilgrims on their way into London could more easily be served.

St Mary Spital was founded by a group of London citizens, in particular Walter and Rose Brown. Walter was a sheriff in the City government and so an important official. They and their associates decided to use their wealth and land to help the poor and the sick living in London. They also believed that by making charitable donations they would be more likely to be accepted into heaven rather than consigned to the horrors of hell. St Mary

Spital was not only a hospital but also a fully-fledged priory with its own prior and canons.

Few remains of this first hospital have been found but the building probably consisted of a small hall for the sick, which would have looked like the nave of a church with a chapel at one end. These establishments were often for 12 or 13 sick people, reflecting the numbers of Christ and his disciples. Documents tell us that the hospital also looked after women in childbirth and cared for their children up to the age of seven, if the women died during childbirth but the children survived.

In 1235 the founders of St Mary Spital issued a new charter, which showed that they had acquired new lands for the hospital. By this time the hospital covered about 13 acres or nearly 5 hectares in area.

D I S C O V E R Y

One of the most remarkable discoveries on site was of the charnel house – a building for storing bones. Documents told us that the building had existed and, from looking at maps of the 1680s, we could guess where the building might be. But how well did it survive? We knew medieval walls on the site could often survive close beneath the ground surface but we could have had no idea of the extraordinary survival of this monument.

As we cleared away the late 17th- and 18th-century soil, which had been dumped throughout Spitalfields, we became increasingly anxious as we approached the probable site of the charnel house. We cleared the area with great care and then a wall began to emerge. Was this the building we had been looking for? It turned out to be one corner of the charnel house and its top was, literally, directly underneath the old road surface, which, because of the camber of the road, was at an extraordinarily high level. We cleared along the rest of the southern wall, taking care neither to disturb any of the walls nor to expose too much of the height of the walls in case they collapsed from the weight of soil behind.

BELOW FROM LEFT The charnel house with a gallery for the Lord Mayor and a tomb, perhaps that of Johanna Eynsham (foreground); the Norwich Cathedral charnel house; the south wall of the charnel house at Spitalfields; recording the central vault with its characteristic, late 12th-century, chevron moulded vaulting rib reused from an earlier building; bones that were left behind when the charnel house was cleared RIGHT Detail of one of the moulded ribs

The interior was particularly difficult to clear. We knew the building had once had a chapel above the charnel house, so might we still have an intact vault? As we cleared away the modern material, elements of the vault began to appear. After a while it became clear that the vault had in fact been deliberately collapsed but that we had much of the stonework. The intact parts of vault that remained were still left attached to the walls of the building. Once we had removed the stone we continued down through the later use of the building to well below the medieval ground level, proving that this was partly an underground crypt. We could now see the slots in the walls where timber stairs had once led down into the crypt from a blocked-in doorway. We realised that the surface we had reached was only the level of the building when it was turned into a house in about 1540. The new owners of the house had built a fireplace against one wall and converted one bay into a chimney. So we continued to dig down, now revealing stone stairs and, in one corner, all that remained of the bones that had once been stored there. By this time we had to have scaffolding built against the south wall to retain it and the remaining vaults were supported to stop them collapsing.

The final discoveries give us a more real and personal picture of the builders of the charnel house. In the soil at the base of the building lay a cracked vaulting rib, which had obviously fallen out whilst it was being erected and was sufficiently damaged not to be reused. We also found the metal end of a builder's spade whose handle may have broken. Perhaps the builder threw it away in a fit of anger.

The precinct

St Mary Spital was divided into several different parts: the infirmaries for the sick; the cloister for the Augustinian canons; an area for the lay sisters who looked after the sick; gardens; orchards; the cemetery; houses for residents; and open land. Whilst we might imagine monasteries to be quiet, calm places, St Mary Spital would have been a bustling place with many hundreds of people living in it.

The visitor entered the hospital through a gate from the main street. A gatekeeper or porter vetted all those who came in, particularly the sick, to make sure, for instance, that there were no lepers amongst them. Once through the gate, the visitor entered a yard and ahead lay the church which was entered through its own porch. To the left lay the hospital infirmaries and to the right a lane that led to the cemetery and the southern part of the hospital precincts.

A second gate into the precincts from the street led into the service yard where there were barns, a brew house for brewing ale, a bake house for making bread and various other outbuildings. The kitchen lay on the other side of the yard, next to where the monastic canons ate, and close to the infirmary.

The gate to St John's Hospital, Canterbury. No doubt this would have been very similar to the gatehouse to St Mary Spital (E W Haslehust)

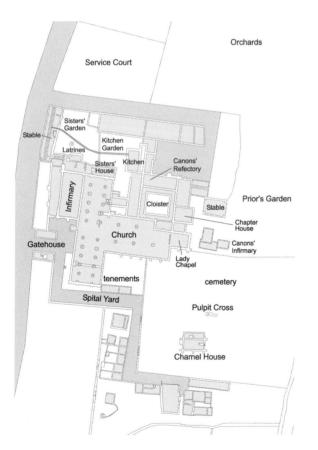

Life in a medieval hospital

What was a medieval hospital like? It was certainly not what we would imagine a hospital to be today. In the main, hospitals provided spiritual and nursing care – the canons (or monks) provided the spiritual care and lay sisters (modern day nurses) looked after the sick. The hospital inmates were laid in beds against the walls, with a central area for the sisters to move around in. Wards for men and women were kept apart. All in all, the layout of the hospital was not that different from one we would see today except that chapels or the main church were linked to the wards, so that the inmates could see religious services being performed.

The inmates were probably fed soup and bread, sometimes accompanied by fish and meat. The sisters would often have served food to the inmates in their beds, on wooden bowls and plates. The inmates may also have had their own lockers in which to keep their personal belongings. A group of small keys found discarded in the infirmary may once have been the keys to such lockers. The beds were probably simply mattresses filled with straw and covered with linen sheets. Lamps, either ceramic or glass oil lamps or metal candleholders, were hung between the beds to provide light.

CLOCKWISE FROM TOP RIGHT
A group of small keys discarded in about 1280 when the infirmary was converted into a chapel – these keys may have been for lockers and appeared to have been thrown away in a box which had rotted; a pair of leather boots discarded outside the infirmary in about 1280; a group of wooden bowls and plates thrown away in the same pit as the leather boots – wooden vessels were extremely common in the medieval period but rarely survive unless they have been discarded in waterlogged ground; two gold rings – the upper plain ring was found in the cemetery, whilst the lower ring, inscribed with the motto 'all my tryst in God', was found in a house near the infirmary

The church

The church was an aisled building, which divided the original infirmary into two parts. The square space between the two wards acted as the nave where the inmates who were mobile, sisters, staff and residents could attend Mass. There would have been no seats for these people and they would have had to stand throughout the service. This nave was divided from the main body of the church to the east, the choir, by the rood screen, so called because it would have had a rood, or statue of the crucified Christ, on it. The choir was the area where the prior and canons celebrated their religious services throughout the day.

LEFT The nave of Lanercost Priory in Cumbria – this Augustinian priory, built at the same time as St Mary Spital, suggests how the inside of St Mary Spital might have looked (Julian Thurgood)
BELOW The walls and foundation of the Lady chapel; in the background are the walls of the canons' dormitory on one side of the cloister

When the old infirmary was replaced in about 1280 by a new two-storey infirmary, the old infirmary was put to a new use as a chapel. Along its eastern wall was a series of chantry chapels with tiled floors. These chantries were designed, as the name suggests, for the names of their founders to be chanted or sung at Masses held in their honour. Medieval Christians from the 13th century onwards believed in the doctrine of purgatory. Essentially this stated that all those who were going to heaven had to endure a period of suffering before reaching heaven to pay for their sins. By building chapels in churches, making charitable donations and paying for Masses, people believed that they could be let off time in purgatory; so the rich were keen to have their praises sung in churches. In some cases the founders of the chapels would be buried in or in front of them in elaborate tombs. Although this was an important part of the attitude to death of people in medieval Christendom, people also believed that only the soul was of importance, not the physical remains of the body.

In about 1400 a new elaborate Lady chapel was added onto the eastern end of the church, the traditional location for Lady chapels. The outside face of the walls was decorated in a pattern of flints and Reigate stone in an attractive chequerboard pattern, common in the period. The inside would have been highly decorated and vividly painted in a way that would look garish to many people's tastes today. One brick tomb in the chapel had been robbed of its skeleton, except for the feet, and reused as a cesspit after the Dissolution. It is possible that this was the tomb of someone whose family wanted him or her to be buried somewhere else, when St Mary Spital was closed and the building knocked down. Perhaps they had the corpse exhumed and then reinterred in another church.

The canons

The cloister lay at the heart of the complex and was surrounded on all sides by the main monastic buildings, which were all built from stone. On the south side lay the church, on the east the chapter house and the dormitory, on the north the refectory and on the west perhaps the prior's lodging and guest accommodation. Many of these buildings were recorded in the 1930s by an archaeologist called Frank Cottrill. We only have his plans of what was found along with some of the decorated floor tiles found in two of the buildings.

The cloister was usually sited on the south side of the church but it was quite common in hospitals and nunneries to place it on the north side. The chapter house was where the main meetings were held between the prior and canons to discuss the daily business of the running of the house, and it occasionally served as the meeting place for the entire Augustinian order. The chapter house was one of the main religious buildings and was consequently one of the most richly ornamented, containing its own decorated tiled floor. The other ground floor rooms were probably used for storage, whilst the upper floor was the dormitory for the canons. This would have had its own access into the cloister via a staircase, with another leading into the church so that the canons could walk straight into the church for the night-time services.

The refectory or dining room was a single-storey building and also had an elaborate decorated tile floor. On one side was a pulpit from which readings were given during meals. North of this building was a small range which may have been the prior's personal apartments in the later medieval period. Next to it was the monastic kitchen where servants prepared the meals.

FAR LEFT An Augustinian canon (The National Gallery, London)
ABOVE Decorated tiles would have been used in the floors of the most important buildings such as the church and the chapter house
BELOW Lanercost Priory and cloister church (Julian Thurgood)

Little is known about the west range of the cloister but traditionally this is the site of the prior's lodging in the earlier medieval period and of accommodation for guests. If it were a two-storey structure, these rooms would have been sited at first-floor level with storerooms beneath.

The square cloister itself had a covered walkway around a central garden. The walkway probably had a vaulted stone ceiling. Fragments of stone recovered suggest the arcade was rebuilt in the 15th century with elaborate tracery and was glazed at this time, presumably with stained glass. This walkway was designed to give the canons access to the main religious buildings and was often used for contemplation. There was usually a sink for washing outside the refectory and some monastic houses had desks, known as carrels, in the cloister where canons could write.

ABOVE Part of a tiled floor in front of a chantry chapel within the church RIGHT The burial of a priest in the cemetery – this man would have been one of the Augustinian canons and was buried with his symbolic communion vessels – a chalice and paten, made from pewter – and these are shown after conservation on the right (unfortunately they can no longer be separated)

The infirmaries

The new infirmary built in the 1230s was designed as a T-shaped building with the infirmaries at right angles to the chapel. Each wing of the infirmary operated as an open ward with 30 beds in each, with the men and women segregated. Each bed had four feet of space: the beds being about two feet wide, with a gap of two feet between them. The main entrance to the infirmary was through the church porch and there was an additional door in the corner of the infirmary, which led into the cemetery. The roof was supported by two rows of graceful circular columns.

In the 1280s a new infirmary was built over the old cemetery and the previous infirmary turned into a large chapel. This new infirmary was larger than the previous one and had two storeys – one floor for men and one for women. The building had a single row of

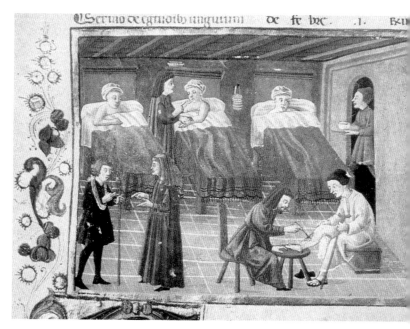

columns down the centre and had room for at
least 40 beds on each floor and more than 60
if beds were laid between the central columns.
Shortly afterwards a new two-storey extension
was added on the west side with room for 22
beds on each floor in a single row against one
of the walls. The latrines lay next to this
extension; they were on two floors, again one
for men and one for women.

Writing some 60 years after the hospital was
closed, John Stow said that the hospital had
180 beds in its infirmary, making it the largest
hospital in London and only rivalled in the
country by St Leonard's in York, which at one
time had 206 inmates. In times of pestilence
two beds were often pushed together and shared
by three people, so St Mary Spital might often
have accommodated more than 200 inmates
in its wards. St Mary's and St Leonard's were,
however, dwarfed by some hospitals on the
Continent: for instance, the great hospital of
Hôtel Dieu in Paris, the modern version of
which still stands next to Nôtre Dame.

The lay sisters

The sisters were employed to look after the sick, carrying out many of the duties associated today with nurses in modern hospitals. They brought food to the sick in their beds, kept the infirmaries tidy and, no doubt, administered poultices and herbal potions, which they may have made up themselves from plants grown in the priory gardens. Documents tell us that there were seven sisters in 1303 but we do not know if there were more at other times. Certainly seven sisters seem few to look after at least 180 inmates at any one time.

Initially they lived in a wooden house in a garden beyond the infirmary. It had a simple mortar floor, which would have been covered in straw and was perhaps roofed in thatch. Eventually a grander, more permanent, stone house was built for them. It had two entrances into their own garden to the north and, presumably, doors into the infirmary, which the house adjoined. At the west end lay their sleeping quarters, which had a porch with an outer door and windows covered by shutters. In the centre of the house was a lobby and on the other side lay a second room, which may have been their dining room. At one end of it lay the foundations of what was perhaps a small dais from which readings could be made at meal times. A door led from the other end to the kitchens.

Scandal was brought upon the priory in the 15th century, when the Bishop of London insisted that a corridor be built up to a window in the kitchen, for the sisters to collect the food for the sick. Evidently they had been consorting with other male members of the priory, conceivably even the canons, and the Bishop wanted to put a stop to it. A wall was then built to separate the sisters' garden from the kitchen garden as a further attempt to keep the sexes apart.

Caring for the sick, as depicted in Bede's Life of St Cuthbert (The British Library)

Food production

With up to 300 people living and working in the precincts, St Mary Spital had many mouths to feed. Much of the food was bought from markets in the city, especially in the 14th and 15th centuries. However, some of the food was produced on the priory's own estates, many of which were in Essex, and some was produced within the precinct. Items such as grain were probably bought and stored in the great barn, and much of its meat was also bought as the animal bone found indicates that the animals were cut up by butchers elsewhere; only the remains of meat joints for eating were present.

The priory had its own orchards and the gardens east of the cloister were full of beds where plants, perhaps vegetables, were grown.

RIGHT A medieval depiction of market traders selling meat (The British Library) BELOW A medieval kitchen garden (The British Library)

There was also a kitchen garden that was probably used for growing herbs. The sisters may have cultivated plants there, or in their own garden, which were used for medicinal purposes.

To the south of the houses around the cemetery, a large ditch separated a big piece of open ground; the ditch was dug to keep animals out of the houses as there was a group of rectangular and circular timber structures which may have been used as animal corrals.

Water supply

One of the most important aspects of any monastic house was its provision of water. Many of the rural monasteries were sited especially with a water supply in mind but this was problematic in an urban setting where space was limited. Water was needed for drinking, cooking, washing, flushing out drains, watering gardens and a host of other jobs.

In 1278, the Bishop of London granted St Mary Spital a well, called Snekockeswell, in the fields east of the priory, with the right for them to pipe this water to the hospital. We have never found any evidence for this water supply but we have found a remarkable reservoir immediately east of the cloister. This was dug down into the water-bearing gravel and had a large wall built to enclose it and separate it from dirty water which was flushed into the northern part from the canons' latrines. This rare find would have held up to 50,000 gallons of water and would have filled up naturally. A hole in the wall acted as an overflow pipe and would also have allowed water to flush away the waste from the drains.

By the later medieval period, this reservoir had been filled in, so the inhabitants of St Mary Spital were presumably relying on the water supply from Snekockeswell and other wells. The sisters had their own well and there was another by the road to the cemetery.

BELOW LEFT The great drain, seen here on the other side of Bishopsgate from St Mary Spital during excavations in 1988 – originally we had thought this drain emptied into a ditch alongside the road

BELOW The reservoir with its stone wall to separate the clean drinking water from the waste water on the other side

The cemetery

There were in fact at least three cemeteries at St Mary Spital, quite apart from the burying space inside the church itself. An early cemetery lay to the south of the 12th-century infirmary and another lay to the west of the 13th-century infirmary. The main cemetery, however, lay to the south-east of the church. It covered an area of about 6000m^2 (about 1.5 acres) and the remains of about 10,500 individuals were found. Later buildings, including the western extension of Spitalfields Market, built in 1928, had destroyed some parts of the cemetery and, indeed, at least 1000 individuals were removed when the Market was built. Analysing the density of burial across the undisturbed areas of the site, we can estimate that at least 18,000 people were once buried in the main cemetery.

ABOVE RIGHT Two skeletons buried in a pit – this pit seems to have been dug originally as a quarry pit and then used for kitchen refuse in the form of oyster shells and for burial

RIGHT A medieval illustration of coffins being interred (Royal Library of Belgium, Brussels, MS 13076 77, fo 24v)

Such a large number of people being buried in the cemetery suggests that St Mary Spital may have acted as an overflow cemetery for London, since there seem to be far too many for people living in the hospital. Some of these people may have wanted to be buried at St Mary Spital or perhaps their parish church had no burial ground. But who else was buried at St Mary Spital? We know that priests from the church were buried there as we find them accompanied by a chalice and paten, their symbolic communion set. We also know that there were benefactors, lay sisters, brethren, staff, priors, lay brothers and residents in houses in the monastery buried there. The benefactors were often buried in tombs in highly visible parts of the cemetery so that they could show off their wealth: two were in front of the charnel house, three in front of the pulpit and two where the road entering the hospital met the cemetery wall. One of these tombs contained the body of a woman, buried with a papal bulla, a lead disc which once accompanied a scroll. These were issued by the Vatican, through the local bishop, as an acknowledgement of an individual's good deeds and were thought to help speed the holder through the horrors of purgatory before reaching heaven. However, we know that many of these were forged and sold, as Chaucer recounts in the Pardoner's Tale.

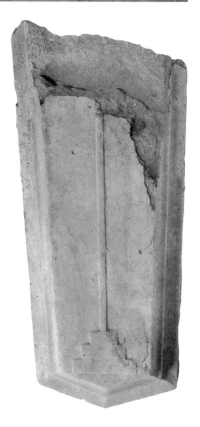

LEFT FROM TOP A papal bulla issued by Pope Innocent VI (1352–62); the papal bulla as found in the hand of a woman; the lower part of a medieval tomb slab – it was reused as the threshold in the late 16th-century rebuilding of the Lord Mayor's gallery
ABOVE The grave of a baby in the cemetery

ABOVE The medieval cemetery looking east – a roof kept excavation of the skeletons hidden from public view and also allowed archaeologists to work in all weathers

RIGHT A tomb in front of the charnel house, possibly that of Johanna Eynsham whom we know was buried in this location in the 1380s or 90s; she and her husband endowed the charnel house with money and had a chantry chapel built there

Most Christians were buried on their backs with their heads to the west so that at the Resurrection they would sit up facing east, towards Jerusalem. However, not everyone was buried like this: occasionally people were buried with their heads to the east (priests were sometimes laid like this in churches so that they would sit up and face their congregation at the Resurrection) and some people were buried face down. These were people who were not going to be resurrected; these included unbaptised children and possibly suicides and murderers.

Perhaps one of the most important discoveries at Spitalfields was a large number of mass burial pits, mostly situated in the southern part of the cemetery. These pits contained multiple layers of skeletons up to five layers deep with up to 45 bodies in a single pit. Contrary to popular belief, in times of famine or epidemic, corpses were not just thrown into hastily dug pits, but were laid with the same reverence and care as in normal times. We are fairly sure that the occupants of each pit died at around the same time and probably represent the death toll for a single

day or week. We also found that many pits were dug through earlier ones, because the gravediggers had run out of space, and that these were excavated only shortly afterwards. So what could be the cause of so many thousands of people dying over what must have been a fairly short period of time? At first, we thought the thousands of people we found must have been the victims of a terrible epidemic, perhaps the Black Death, which first visited England in 1348–9. Radiocarbon dating, however, shows us that these people were buried at some time between 1270 and 1320, which is about half a century too early for them to be victims of the Black Death. Many other theories have been put forward including something as mundane but potentially lethal as flu. At the moment we do not know what these people died of and we may never know. One possibility is that they died of starvation; closer inspection of the bones and teeth may provide us with signs of malnutrition. We know that there were famines in 1294 and in the years between 1310 and 1322 due to poor harvests, and perhaps it was these famines that were responsible for the deaths of the 3000–4000 people who were buried at St Mary Spital. This remains one of the most intriguing questions from the site.

ABOVE The skeleton of a woman with an in utero foetus and three other babies buried around her – this unusual group of burials reminds us of the hospital's function as a lying-in hospital for pregnant women

LEFT One layer of skeletons in a mass burial pit; at the top of the picture are skeletons in an earlier pit which have been cut through by the later pit. There were often four or five layers of skeletons in each pit but they were almost always laid with the same care and reverence as a burial in an individual grave would have been

RADIOCARBON DATING

Because the cemetery contained little in the way of conventional archaeological dating material, like pottery, we were forced to consider other techniques of dating the graves. The answer was to send selected bones for radiocarbon dating by laboratories in Scotland, Northern Ireland and USA.

Radiocarbon dating is not an exact science but does give a range of dates for when living things died. It works on the principle that all things contain a certain proportion of ordinary carbon and radioactive carbon. When a living thing dies the radioactive carbon begins to decay and the rate is known to be 5568 years for half of it to decay. So, the proportion of radioactive carbon to ordinary carbon can be measured and the difference between that and the levels of radioactive carbon to ordinary carbon, which would exist in a living creature, will tell us how long ago it died. Unfortunately, the amounts are very tiny and the levels of radiocarbon do not always seem to have been consistent so we have a range of possible dates that have to be set against a curve to calibrate the dates. This curve is based on dendrochronological dates – tree ring dates – of known trees that have also been radiocarbon dated.

The result has been to give us an accurate chronology for our cemetery – vital if we are to understand the changing population from the 12th to the 16th century.

A medieval cemetery, however, was not just used for burial of the dead. It was also a place for the living, as a cemetery might be today, where people could sit in contemplation, pay their respects to the dead, or take part in mass public meetings. St Mary Spital was a very important place for public gatherings, which were held at a pulpit in the centre of the cemetery. In an age when there were no newspapers or media, pulpits in churches were the only way of informing the public of both religious and political news. Outdoor pulpits were rare and only sited in the most important places. London's most important outdoor pulpit was at St Paul's, in a spot now marked by a cross. The pulpit at St Mary Spital is first mentioned in 1398 when Richard II's proclamations of the

Parliament held at Shrewsbury were read there but it might have been built much earlier. The pulpit was used for yearly sermons held at Easter and regular sermons on Sundays. A sermon was read at St Paul's on Good Friday and then at St Mary Spital on the following Monday, Tuesday and Wednesday. It is easy to imagine thousands of people gathering in front of the pulpit to listen to the speakers.

In 1488 a new building was built onto the side of the charnel house, facing the pulpit. This was a gallery for important members of society to listen to the sermons at the pulpit. It was a two-storey stone house with accommodation for the Lord Mayor and sheriffs of London downstairs and the Bishop of London and other high-ranking ecclesiastics from other monasteries upstairs. It was rebuilt in brick and stone in 1594 with new timber floors and by this time the monasteries had been closed, so the wives of the aldermen and sheriffs used the upstairs. Coins found in the holes left by the rotted floor joists must have been lost by the Lord Mayor and his friends during the speeches. The schoolmasters and children of Christ's Hospital also used to attend the sermons, sitting on specially built stands until they were provided with their own brick house in 1594. Rows of holes where the posts used to be to the south and west of the pulpit show where the temporary stands were. Documents attest to a Thomas Townson, a master carpenter who built one of these stands in 1579.

By 1594 the pulpit was either in a poor state of repair or perhaps it was getting in the way and a new pulpit was built, facing in a different direction. This time it was built from wood, presumably so it could be put up at Easter and

ABOVE A silver ring inscribed with the names of the Biblical three kings was found on the hand of a woman buried in the 14th century and laid on a layer of ashes

LEFT The mass burial pits were found even underneath the charnel house – clear evidence that the building was constructed after whatever had caused thousands to die in a short period of time

RIGHT The foundations of the 14th-century pulpit – the foundation in the foreground was for the stairs. This medieval pulpit was replaced with a timber version in 1598

FAR RIGHT The pulpit at St Paul's surrounded by galleries for dignitaries, as at St Mary Spital, and a churchyard full of the general public (Guildhall Library, Corporation of London)

BELOW A skeleton found beneath the basement of Spitalfields Market with four skulls laid alongside, presumably disturbed by gravediggers

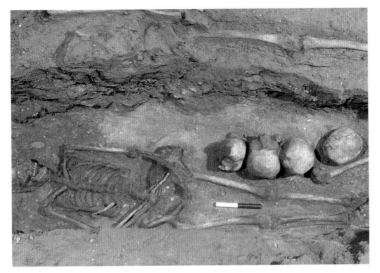

at other times when it was needed and then taken down again afterwards. The holes for the posts could still be seen where they had been cut into the old stone pulpit. We do not know when the pulpit finally went out of use, although we do know that the Puritans pulled down the pulpit at St Paul's in 1643 but that the Spital Cross was still probably in use in 1680. Indeed Pepys records attending the sermons and in 1669 and said that he

heard a piece of a dull sermon to my Lord Mayor and Aldermen, and thence saw them all take horse and ride away, which I have not seen together many a-day; their wives also went in their coaches; and, indeed, the sight was mighty pleasing.

Disease

Despite finding the remains of many thousands of people in the cemetery, in most cases the cause of death will remain unknown because most people die of illness or injury, which affects the organs or tissue, which leave no trace in the ground. However, some diseases do affect the bone and we have found a remarkable number of these. One is tuberculosis, although the disease only affects the skeleton in less than 5% of cases. So we can assume that about 20 times as many people were actually suffering from tuberculosis as we can see in the skeletons. In total we have found at least 75 people whose skeletons showed signs of tuberculosis, which suggests that more than 1500 were suffering from the disease. Tuberculosis is a disease associated with poverty and poor living conditions, and

ABOVE A medieval depiction of a bishop attempting to cure plague victims
LEFT Laying out bones to dry after washing
BELOW Upper part of spine showing classic signs of tuberculosis

needs a large densely packed population to grow. Interestingly, at least three people who had leprosy were buried at St Mary Spital, despite the statutes explicitly banning them from the hospital. Two were buried in mass burial pits, suggesting that they were perhaps not residents, whilst the third was buried in the 14th or 15th century at the southern limit of the cemetery. Perhaps this latter person, a woman, was also not a resident at the hospital or did the gatekeeper miss her symptoms when she was admitted?

There are many other ailments which can be seen on the skeleton including arthritis, syphilis and a disease known as diffuse idiopathic skeletal hyperostosis, commonly known as DISH. This was a disease that affected people who had very rich diets and it is often associated with those who were wealthy – perhaps the clergy or benefactors. Because people lived to a lesser age, in general, in the medieval period, cancer is a rare find in an archaeological skeleton and so far we have only one example, although we may yet find others.

Many congenital or inherited diseases were also seen, including individuals with a club foot or a cleft lip. Not surprisingly for a population of the poor, there were a few examples of people who had diseases related to vitamin deficiency, such as rickets and scurvy, although these were much more rare than one might expect. Perhaps the diet of poor Londoners was not so bad as we might think. There were also fewer of the 'lifestyle diseases' such as those relating to alcohol, tobacco and sugar than there are today; the generally good teeth are a clear indication of the lack of sugar in the diet.

COLUMBUS AND SYPHILIS

Syphilis is one of the treponemal type diseases and is a disease that, because it affects the bones, can be readily identified on human skeletons. One skull, disturbed when Spitalfields Market was extended in the 1920s, had already been identified as having syphilis but no one knew when the person had died. Preliminary work on the bones from the site has identified at least 36 cases of treponemal disease. This is a very large number, although it represents only a tiny proportion of the people buried in the cemetery.

Previous writers had concluded that syphilis had been brought back to Europe by Columbus and his army, after they had conquered the New World at the end of the 15th century. It was thought that they had caught it from the local indigenous peoples and that once back it had spread quickly throughout Europe. Some writers were challenging this theory but could we prove it?

One of our skeletons was that of a child with syphilis, which we knew must have been passed on from its mother and thus must have been the sexually transmitted variety of the disease. The child lay in a pit with other skeletons and, since we did not want to destroy any of the bone from this skeleton, we radiocarbon dated a bone from a skeleton which immediately overlay it in the pit, knowing that the child with syphilis must, therefore, have been buried earlier even if only by a matter of hours. The radiocarbon date we got back was 1273–1300, thus proving that syphilis was not brought back by Columbus and his followers but had much earlier roots in Europe.

LEFT Bones with classic signs of treponemal disease

Medicine

Medieval people did not understand the idea of infectious disease. However, they do seem to have equated foul smells with something being not quite right. This is clear from many monastic houses and is equally true at St Mary Spital, since they cleaned their drains out scrupulously, maintained excellent water supplies and kept the two well apart. This is in marked contrast with later Spitalfields where drains were clogged with sewage, and cesspits and wells were often dug no more than a few feet apart.

Medieval hospitals rarely employed doctors because they worked privately and were very expensive. However, sometimes people might leave money in their wills as a charitable gift for doctors to visit and work at hospitals. Money was left in 1455 for a surgeon called Thorneton to work at St Mary Spital and a number of other hospitals, and there was a Dr Smith living in the house next to the infirmary in the 16th century. We do not know for certain, however, whether either actually practised at the hospital.

Mostly, the lay sisters would have provided nursing care for the sick and perhaps used herbal remedies for their ailments. There are many natural plants used for their medicinal properties, which have been found in soil samples from St Mary Spital. These include cannabis, opium, cabbage, mallow and

CLOCKWISE FROM TOP LEFT The drain exiting the cloister, probably from the canons' latrines; the infirmary latrines which were flushed out under Bishopsgate to the River Walbrook; a medieval dentist extracting teeth using a cord (The British Library)

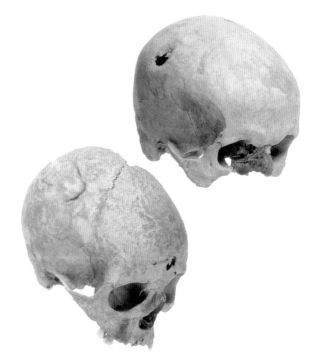

henbane. Wild cabbage was used to relieve the symptoms of, amongst other things, gout and rheumatism, and mallow for making poultices, whilst the other three were more powerful narcotics widely used for relieving pain.

We also know from the skeletons that other surgical practices were carried out, although we cannot be sure that they happened at St Mary Spital. Two skeletons were found with pieces of metal attached to their legs, perhaps as some kind of support. One had two copper plates tied around his knee with a piece of textile, whilst the other had a sheet of lead wrapped around his lower leg. There were also high numbers of skeletons with healed fractures of various bones but mostly leg and arm bones. Use of splints is well documented and the sisters would almost certainly have been able to carry out relatively simple procedures such as these. A broken limb could always get infected and the patient might die.

Examples of more serious forms of surgery include individuals with amputated limbs and skulls that had been trepanned. Trepanning was a form of surgery, still used today, which involved drilling a hole through the skull to release pressure on the brain. It was thought to be a cure for madness. All the individuals who had been trepanned had survived their ordeal as the bone had started to heal over again.

Even quite serious injuries seem not to have necessarily resulted in death. One person had three wounds to the skull, which may have been caused by an axe or sword, but all had had time to heal. This person certainly seems to have been the victim of a violent assault, possibly even in a battle.

It was care for the soul, however, that was considered to be the most important aspect of care at a medieval hospital. Spiritual care, decent food and nursing care were the staple diet for the inmates in a medieval hospital.

ABOVE Excavating a skeleton with the right leg amputated below the knee

ABOVE RIGHT Two skulls, one with a trepanning hole which has partly healed over, the other from the victim of a serious assault; the cuts in the skull resulted from blows with an axe or sword

RIGHT A medieval depiction of head surgery (The British Library)

RECORDING THE BURIALS

Knowing that we were going to find many thousands of burials gave us a few logistical headaches, of which the biggest was how to record them. Archaeologists draw scale plans of everything they find, so that afterwards they can locate all the buildings, yards, pits and graves. Burials have always been the most time-consuming archaeological find to draw and often they require people with high quality drafting skills if they are to look like skeletons afterwards. Normally archaeologists might plan one or perhaps two skeletons in a day – imagine having to plan 10,500! Other techniques used had been to photograph them from directly overhead with known points in the photograph and then draw them up from scaled photographs later. This saved time on site but was still enormously costly and time consuming afterwards.

However, technology came to our rescue and we decided that we would survey all the skeletons. We had teams of surveyors: one looked through a surveying instrument, which was set up over a known point, whilst another held a prism over each of the main bones of the skeleton. The surveying instrument sends out a beam that is reflected back by the prism, telling the surveyor exactly where the point surveyed is to the nearest millimetre. Using a hand-held computer, the surveyor can then join up the dots to produce an accurate diagrammatic plan of the skeleton. With this system, the surveyors could record 25 skeletons a day between two of them, instead of one or two. This not only saved a huge amount of time and money but also ensured that every plan was perfectly located.

Houses

Having entered the main gate to St Mary Spital, a lane (now Spital Yard) led off to the right into the southern part of the precinct and the cemetery. Alongside this gravel track lay a row of timber-framed houses with stone foundations. Some of these houses had their own gardens with chalk-lined cesspits for disposal of their waste. Who lived in these houses?

They were mostly built in the 14th century and were used for a variety of different functions. We know that the ground floor of one was used for ironworking, from the large hearth and all the iron waste on the floor. Another had a small glass vessel containing mercury buried in the floor. All were probably of two storeys and most had a view looking across the cemetery. They were all floored simply in mortar or clay, which would have been covered in straw. We know that the house

TOP RIGHT A hearth made from pitched roof tiles; the tiles at the back were to protect the wooden walls from catching fire

RIGHT A large cesspit, where waste could be thrown away, in one of the back gardens to the houses

BELOW The hearth in the corner of an ironworker's workshop

near the church was at one time lived in by Joan Rosse and we also know the names of others who lived in the precincts, for instance Lady Cecilia Kyryell, Lord Hugh Capell, the Bishop of Chichester and Sir Henry Plesyngton, who was later buried in the church. One other tenant of St Mary Spital's – either in the precinct or just outside in Bishopsgate – was a prostitute called Joan Jolybody! This is not exactly the kind of profession that most of us would associate with a monastic house. But it does show what a cosmopolitan and secular place a medieval monastery and its surroundings was, and that our preconceptions of religious fervour and quiet peace and calm may not be quite as accurate as we suppose.

We also know something of the lifestyles of these people from the bones and seeds that we find, as well as from the documents. We know that people ate a lot of cereals and bread; we also know that they ate a variety of meat, primarily beef and mutton, but also a little goose, duck and chicken. The animals were not, however, the young animals we are used to but older cattle with many years of producing milk or old sheep that had been used for producing wool. Fish was regularly eaten, both freshwater and saltwater; plaice and herrings seem to have been the most popular. Since water was not always suitable for drinking, people would often drink something known as 'small beer', which was very weak alcoholic ale. One former prior, Robert de Cerne, who was deposed for, amongst other things, allowing the canons to consort with prostitutes in the precinct, was given a chamber near the infirmary and a canon to watch over him. He was given an allowance of food that included a double issue of bread, ale and cooked food, and another issue of food for a servant boy.

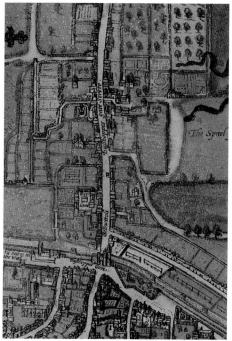

ABOVE The foundations of some of the houses south of the cemetery; the road and cemetery lay to the right of the photograph

LEFT A detail from Braun and Hogenburg's map of 1572 showing the former precinct of St Mary Spital

FAR LEFT Medieval butchers cutting up meat (The British Library)

One fine building originally contained a cellar built from chalk, which was entered down a flight of wooden steps. This, along with most of the other houses, was demolished and the owner of this particular house left behind two hoards of coins, one a rare group of gold coins, known as 'angels', from the reign of Henry VIII.

The inhabitants of these houses were probably a mixture of people: from the wealthy who wanted a secluded London town house; to artisans who rented space to live and work; to the elderly or widowed who wanted a quiet place to which they could retire. We must also remember that by the later medieval period, say the middle of the 14th century, the idea that people should donate money to provide charity for the poor was changing to one where the emphasis was on charity for the 'deserving poor'. Thus almshouses and hospitals were founded for blind priests, retired seamen or elderly members of City guilds. Perhaps St Mary Spital was also trying to cater for these people as well as continuing to maintain its facilities for the general sick poor; they certainly built an almshouse for just these sorts of people, north of the hospital, in the late medieval period.

ABOVE A window shutter with hinges discarded in a pit – only the grandest buildings had glass in their windows; most simply had shutters like this one

FAR RIGHT FROM TOP A group of seven gold coins known as 'angels' dating to 1509–26 – the time of Henry VIII. Their owner must have lost these when the houses were demolished in around 1538; a chalk cellar with its doorway on the right-hand side – this was originally reached by a flight of wooden stairs; a circular kiln in one of the houses

RIGHT Two medieval stone lamps with coats of arms carved on each side; these would have held oil with a floating wick

The canons' infirmary

By 1400 the canons at St Mary Spital had their own infirmary so that they could rest somewhere when they were sick away from the hustle and bustle of the public infirmary. This consisted of a rectangular building with a kitchen attached on the north side. It may have been that the sick canons were allowed a more relaxed diet with a wider range of foods, which were cooked in the adjoining kitchen. In its centre was a large rectangular hearth surrounded by posts, which supported a spit for roasting meats.

The infirmary itself would have been laid out in the same way as the public infirmary, with beds laid against the walls, but in this case the building only had to accommodate a maximum of 12 people, if all the canons were sick at the same time. No doubt the prior would have been attended in his own private quarters. As time went on, small rooms were added onto the side of the infirmary, which may indicate a phenomenon seen widely at other religious houses. Originally the monastic rule ordered that the monks or canons should live communally but it is clear that by the latter part of the medieval period, dormitories and infirmaries were divided by screens to give the monks or canons more privacy.

RIGHT In the kitchen (bottom right of the picture) food for the sick was prepared over a central hearth; the canons' infirmary (top right) was where the canons were looked after when they were sick; the building centre left was perhaps where the infirmarer brewed his potions

ABOVE LEFT Hearths in the building next to the canons' infirmary covered almost half the floor area and ceramic vessels found discarded in a pit outside may have been used for making medicines; was this building where the infirmarer brewed potions for sick monks?

FAR LEFT A 14th-century curcurbit or distillation vessel found in a pit outside the canon's infirmary

LEFT A room added on to the infirmary was equipped with its own hearth to keep the room warm and may have given a sick canon more privacy

RIGHT The kitchen with its central hearth. The blackened material that gathered on the floor stopped in a line short of the walls, suggesting that the walls were once lined with wooden cupboards

Attached to the end of the infirmary was one other extraordinary building. It was quite small but almost half its floor was covered in hearths made from pitched tiles. What was going on in this building? Obviously large fires were required so perhaps some industrial or even medicinal practices were carried out here. In a pit outside of the building was a large group of unusual ceramic and glass vessels, some of which appear to be for distillation, whilst others are parts of large tripods for putting over fires to support other vessels containing whatever was being heated up. Initial study of the remains from these vessels shows that metals such as mercury, iron, copper and arsenic were being heated up; this suggests to us that they may have been making medicines in this building.

The end – Reformation and Dissolution

On January 1st 1539 the Priory and Hospital of St Mary Spital was finally closed by order of Henry VIII. The hospital, along with all the monasteries of England and Wales, was dissolved as a consequence of the Reformation. Henry had made himself head of the English Church and cut England off from Catholicism. The power of the monastic houses was seen as being tied up with the Papacy and the religious orders on the Continent and they were also a symbol of the corruption which many saw in the church. In addition they were the source of very great wealth, which Henry coveted.

The almshouses built for specific sections of the community survived the Dissolution, as they were essentially secular in character, often run by guilds or town authorities. The great hospitals for the sick and the poor, however, were not so fortunate. The closure of these hospitals throughout England must have had a catastrophic effect on the care for the poor, the needy and the sick – where were they to go and who was going to look after them? The Lord Mayor of London, Sir Richard Gresham, sent a petition to Henry VIII in August 1538 asking him to hand over the hospitals of St Mary Spital, St Thomas, St Bartholomew and the Abbey of St Mary Graces to the City authorities, so that they could continue to provide much needed succour to the poor. The petition was rejected although the sick were allowed to remain in the hospital wards at St Mary Spital until they either died or recovered. On the other hand, Gresham also wrote in that same month in response to the collapse of part of the church roof that '...it was the will of God that

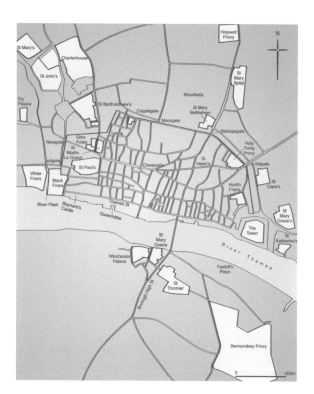

LEFT Religious houses around the City of London
ABOVE Two medieval column bases and an associated column, reused in a house wall
RIGHT A reconstruction of St Mary Spital on the eve of the Dissolution, viewed from the north-west, produced after the excavations of the 1980s; comparison with the reconstruction on page 30 shows how much we have learnt about the hospital in the last few years (Kikar Singh)

RIGHT St Bartholomew's priory church – part of the priory and hospital founded in the 12th century; the nave was demolished at the Dissolution and this view shows the crossing, now the west end of the present church

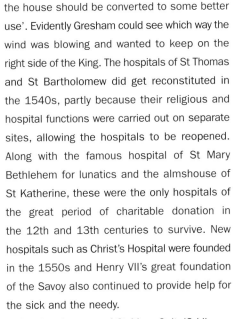

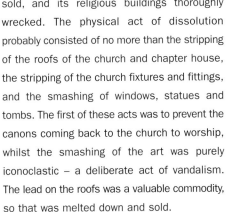

the house should be converted to some better use'. Evidently Gresham could see which way the wind was blowing and wanted to keep on the right side of the King. The hospitals of St Thomas and St Bartholomew did get reconstituted in the 1540s, partly because their religious and hospital functions were carried out on separate sites, allowing the hospitals to be reopened. Along with the famous hospital of St Mary Bethlehem for lunatics and the almshouse of St Katherine, these were the only hospitals of the great period of charitable donation in the 12th and 13th centuries to survive. New hospitals such as Christ's Hospital were founded in the 1550s and Henry VII's great foundation of the Savoy also continued to provide help for the sick and the needy.

So what became of St Mary Spital? Like so many religious houses the site was valued and sold, and its religious buildings thoroughly wrecked. The physical act of dissolution probably consisted of no more than the stripping of the roofs of the church and chapter house, the stripping of the church fixtures and fittings, and the smashing of windows, statues and tombs. The first of these acts was to prevent the canons coming back to the church to worship, whilst the smashing of the art was purely iconoclastic – a deliberate act of vandalism. The lead on the roofs was a valuable commodity, so that was melted down and sold.

The site was then split in two. The church, cemetery and all the northern parts of the precinct were leased to a variety of individuals before finally coming under the ownership of Stephen Vaughan. The southern parts of the precinct were leased by the prior of St Mary Spital on 3 January 1538 to the 'fraternity or guild of artillery of longbows, crossbows and handguns', a year before the Dissolution; by this time he could see the fate awaiting his monastery.

THE ARTILLERY GROUND

The Honourable Artillery Company

The identity of the 'fraternity or guild of artillery of longbows, crossbows and handguns', also known as the 'fraternity of St George', to whom the prior leased the artillery ground, has never been established. It was the root of a long-running and bitter dispute between the two organisations that came to the use the Artillery Ground – the Honourable Artillery Company and the Gunners of the Tower – since neither of them could prove they had the sole rights to the land. It is probable, however, that the fraternity was the forerunner of the Honourable Artillery Company. When the priory was dissolved the land became the property of the Crown and remained so until it was sold in 1682. In 1538, when the prior leased out the Artillery Ground, the priory had built a new brick wall along three of its sides leaving only the north side open, although this was also eventually enclosed.

The Honourable Artillery Company is the oldest regiment in the British Army but has been a Territorial regiment for about the last 100 years. Before the company finally moved to its current site at Bunhill Fields in 1658, it occupied the southern end of the Artillery Ground and built a range of buildings there, including storehouses and an armoury. The company originally practised with the crossbow but eventually practised firing small arms and, after many disputes, was allowed to train on the cannon along the firing range.

The skeletons of two men who died at some time during the 17th century were found in the Artillery Ground. Unusually these were buried north–south rather than east–west, which tells us that they were probably Dissenters or Puritans.

LEFT The Honourable Artillery Company at Bunhill Fields as painted by Albert Henry Payne in 1893 (Corporation of London)

RIGHT The brick wall around the Artillery Ground

The Gunners of the Tower

The Gunners of the Tower (of London) were using the Artillery Ground for artillery practice only once a year in 1581 but by 1598 they were practising there weekly. This was the era of conflict between England and Spain, although most of that was at sea. The Master Gunner of England trained scholars in gunnery there and up to 100 gunners also practised there regularly. The trained bands of London and Middlesex, local groups of people who trained in arms and artillery in their spare time, so that they could be called upon in times of need, also practised there. Small arms, crossbows and guns, were fired at targets in the ground but the large artillery was fired down a range about 200m long on the eastern side of the ground. At the other end of the range was a large butt of earth – the target – and it was perhaps from this that a cannonball was found when Spitalfields Market was extended in 1928. Alongside this range were the powder houses, separated from the range by a row of trees, but nonetheless a dangerous place for the powder stores if a cannon was fired off target. Next to the powder houses was a large pond, presumably to hold water to put out any fires. Pepys describes going to the Artillery Ground in 1669 to view a new gun being tested:

> *I did go to see his new gun tryed, this being the place where the Officers of the Ordnance do try all their great guns; and when we come, did find that the trial had been made; and they going away with extraordinary report of the proof of his gun, which, from the shortness and bigness, they do call Punchinello.*

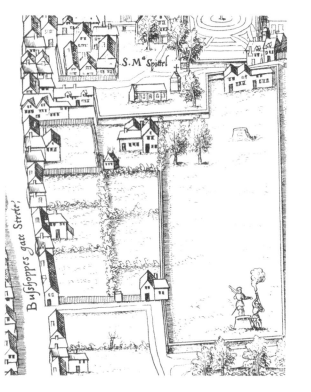

ABOVE Musket balls and shot were found throughout the Artillery Ground; targets were set up across the ground for people to practise with small arms

LEFT The copperplate map of the 1550s showing the gunners firing in the Artillery Ground (bottom right), the charnel house and pulpit (centre), and beyond the former monastic buildings now converted into houses

BELOW LEFT Samuel Pepys, who visited the Artillery Ground in 1669

We know the names of a number of the Master Gunners of England, including William Hammond, James Wemyss and Captain Valentine Pyne. At least the last two of these lived in a house in the Artillery Ground called the Master Gunner of England's house. This was built before 1645 and was a fine brick house of two storeys or more with tiled floors – the sort lived in by a wealthy member of the establishment. The entrance hall led into rooms on one side of the house that were probably for servants, whilst the other side had a large room with a fireplace that was obviously the main room in the house. Another smaller room may have been a study or withdrawing room and this even contained the remains of timber panelling on the walls. At the far end lay a brick cellar at the base of which were two sealed wine bottles, which still contained their

original contents. One of these was tested and found to contain Madeira, a highly expensive wine, which, at that time, was not a fortified wine. The Master Gunner must have left the bottles on the floor when he vacated the house in 1682, when the land was sold.

Two other buildings included a house with a fine tiled floor and a proving house for testing guns. The first of these buildings was evidently a house of some importance as it had a floor of tiles, which had been reused from the old priory, and a fireplace made from carved stones from the demolished buildings.

ABOVE A late 17th-century bottle, still with its original contents, found in the Master Gunner's cellar
RIGHT Extracting the contents of the bottle for testing – the bottle was found to contain Madeira

Cottage industries

The ground as originally let was known as the 'Teasel Ground', presumably because teasels (a plant used for brushing up the nap on cloth) grew there. Not only did gunners practise artillery there but people were also carrying out a variety of small cottage industries on the site. This sounds as if it might have been extremely hazardous but there are no recorded accidents and perhaps in the early days the artillery was practised separately to the industry.

A kiln or clamp, as they were known, may have been used for making the bricks for the new brick wall around the Artillery Ground. This temporary structure would have been used only until the supplies of the natural subsoil, brickearth, had been used up or, in this case, until sufficient bricks had been made. The new brick wall was built with small niches, perhaps either for keeping bees or for placing small candles.

LEFT A teasel, used to raise the nap on cloth
BELOW LEFT The remains of a brick or tile kiln; perhaps this kiln made the bricks for the new wall around the Artillery Ground
BELOW This niche in the wall may have been used for keeping bees or perhaps holding lamps

MOOR FIELD.

CLOCKWISE FROM ABOVE

Some of the many lead seals found in the Artillery Ground – these would have been attached to cloth to authenticate the product; workers laying out cloths to dry in Moorfields (taken from the copperplate map of the 1550s); cow metatarsals or knucklebones thrown into a shallow gully in the Artillery Ground; cow metatarsals were used by pinners to sharpen pins – hence the grooves down the bones; a combination bone knife and flute dating to the 17th century

The numerous bedding trenches across the western part of the ground show that local people were growing plants in the area, perhaps the teasels after which the site was known. The large number of cloth seals – lead marks denoting the authenticity and quality of cloth – also found here suggests that this part of the ground was used as a tenter ground: that is that cloths were laid out and stretched on the ground, whilst teasels were used for raising the nap on the cloth.

Local workers in the area were also using the remains of butchered cattle. The knuckles or metapodials were cut off the slaughtered animals and used in one instance for laying a floor, whilst other bones had grooves down their sides showing that they were used for making pins. Many of these industries were incredibly simple and, in the case of pin makers, were carried out by some of the poorest members of society, desperate to make a living.

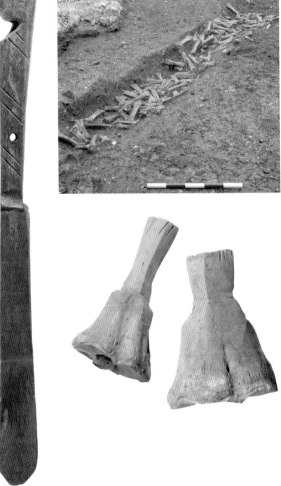

DISCOVERY

One of the most unexpected discoveries on the site was a fort dating to the period of the English Civil War. The Civil War defences around London are mapped and their locations reasonably well known, but archaeologists have been looking for them with limited success and it was remarkable that we should find defences of this date in such an unexpected place.

Initially we found a large V-shaped ditch about 4m wide and 2m deep – interesting and involving a huge amount of work to excavate but not exactly earth-shattering. As we began to clear it, however, it became clear that the southern part of it was 'star-shaped' in plan: a classic design of English forts in the 17th century. This design evolved as a means of defending castles and forts against artillery. It soon became clear to engineers of the time that straight stone walls were no defence against cannon, so round stone forts were developed in Henry VIII's time to defend England's southern coast. Round forts had the disadvantage for the defenders, however, of them not being able to fire along the walls at attackers attempting to scale them and, in any case, stone shatters badly under artillery bombardment.

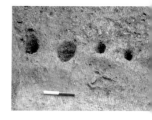

ABOVE Holes inside the Civil War ditch where wooden stakes would have been set; these might possibly have been sharpened to impale onrushing attackers

BELOW FROM LEFT Excavating the fort ditch; the darker line at the base of the ditch shows where an earlier version of the ditch had been dug and

backfilled; the western half of the fort – the outlines of some of the medieval houses, cut through by the ditch, can also be made out; reconstruction of the area in around 1640, showing the fort in the foreground, the earls of Bolingbroke's house in the centre and the 'Principal Tenement' to its right (Faith Vardy); an aerial view of Tilbury Fort which was built in the late 17th century, showing the classic 'star-shaped' design (English Heritage)

So Dutch engineers designed forts with plenty of straight sides so that defenders could fire along them, lots of angles to provide cover for defenders, earth walls which absorbed the impact of cannon and a deep wide ditch in front of the earth walls for the attackers to get across.

We had, in fact, seen tiny parts of the fort during works in 1991 and 1996 without realising what they were. As we removed the infills of the ditch we found numerous holes where wooden posts had once been set on the insides of the ditch. Some of these holes were vertical, indicating that the posts had been supports for an earth bank on the inside of the ditch, and others were at 45°, indicating that they had contained sharpened stakes, which onrushing attackers would have impaled themselves upon as they poured into the ditch.

The final discovery came from the dating of the infills of the ditch. Pottery and, especially, clay pipes indicated that the bank surrounding the ditch had been pushed back in some time in the early 1640s and we could tell that the ditch had not been open for long. Thus we could conclude that this was the first fort dating to the English Civil War to be excavated in London. Whether it was a real fort defending part of the Artillery Ground, or whether it was a practice fort in preparation for building London's defences, remains open to question.

THE ENGLISH CIVIL WAR

The English Civil War was fought, largely from 1640–5, between the royalists (forces loyal to the king) and the Parliamentarians. The origins of the dispute went back over many years but ultimately were centred around King Charles I's refusal to accede to the will of Parliament and his belief in the divine right of the king to decide on any matter. Such was his belief in this that when Parliament defied him, he closed Parliament down.

The War was fought right across England; it split communitites and even families. Not only were there pitched battles, such as those at Edgehill, Naseby and Marston Moor, but sieges to most of the great cities. The only city that was not put under siege was London, which was a staunchly Parliamentarian city. Charles set up his headquarters in Oxford. However, this did not stop the authorities building defences around London, as London's inhabitants were, not surprisingly, very concerned that Charles I might wish to attack and take the capital city. An enormous ditch and earth bank was constructed right around London with forts at all the major junctions with roads. The defences were much further out than the old city walls, showing just how much London had expanded and also that the authorities were keen to include agricultural land, to provide food, within the defences.

ABOVE A map of the Civil War defences around London, built during the 1640s
LEFT Portrait of Oliver Cromwell by Peter Lely in about 1654

After the battle of Edgehill in 1642, a draw between the two armies but with the Royalists gaining the upper hand, Charles and his army marched as far as Turnham Green on the outskirts of west London today. Had he pressed on, the course of the war and English history might have changed forever, but Charles turned back and London was never threatened again, although Londoners did try to prevent a Parliamentarian army entering the City in 1647. The defences proved no match for the attackers, however, and within four days they were overrun. Shortly afterwards the Parliamentarians had the banks and forts flattened, and the ditches filled in, so that Londoners could not defy them again.

Once Charles had retreated from London the course of the Civil War tended to go against the Royalists. They had some successes with captures of cities such as Bristol and the winning of some minor skirmishes but in the end the Royalists were conclusively beaten at the major battles at Naseby in 1644 and Marston Moor in 1645 by Oliver Cromwell's 'New Model Army' – the first professional trained army in England. For a few more years, the Parliamentarians prevaricated as to Charles' fate but finally put him on trial for treason in January 1649 and executed him, thus bringing in the Commonwealth until 1660 when the monarchy was restored under Charles II.

BELOW Pikemen in a modern Civil War re-enactment (Nigel Hillyard)

BELOW RIGHT A painting of Charles I after his execution, with his head stitched back on. The three distressed women to the right depict the crowns falling from England, Scotland and Ireland

FROM ARISTOCRATIC ENCLAVE TO SUBURB OF IMMIGRANTS

Stephen Vaughan's house

After the Dissolution the main precincts of St Mary Spital went through a number of hands before they came into the ownership of Stephen Vaughan. Vaughan worked for the Court of Augmentations, which was responsible for handing out the former monastic precincts. Many went to wealthy aristocrats or members of the Court of Augmentations themselves, which gives a clear picture of the culture of cronyism prevalent at the time. For instance, the priory at Bermondsey went to Sir Thomas Pope, the nunnery at Clerkenwell to the Duke of Newcastle and the Charterhouse to the Duke of Norfolk.

When Vaughan moved in, he occupied the old canons' dormitory on the east side of the cloister and the refectory on the north. These buildings probably remained relatively unchanged until they were demolished around 1700. He had the north and south walls of the church demolished and their stone was reused for new buildings, leaving him with a large garden, which occupied the former cloister and the church. He also had a drain built from his house to a cesspit, which reused some of the old foundations of the church.

Many of the other buildings were left standing and rented out, with some retaining the same tenants as before the Dissolution, such as Joan Rosse in a house on the south side of the old church. These houses remained as stone founded, half-timbered buildings, although by about 1600 many occupiers were beginning to alter and improve their buildings, often in brick.

LEFT The cellar floor of a late 17th-century house

RIGHT A large new brick house east of the former cloister

Facing Vaughan's House across a narrow lane was one of the grandest of the new brick houses. The builders had to construct deep arched foundations to support the building over the marshy ground, which had once been the reservoir, but even this did not prevent some of the walls from slumping. This was a multi-roomed house with brick floors and fireplaces, and adjoining cesspits. One of the floors had a pot set into it, perhaps to catch water on the floor. The house was probably of at least three storeys and had ample gardens behind it. The northern part of the old reservoir was progressively infilled and timber revetments built to retain the land.

The old precincts of St Mary Spital became the residences of a number of members of the

minor aristocracy and well to do in the 16th century but, as the population of London grew, cheaper housing in the area was built to accommodate these new people. Many of the early inhabitants were Catholics who were still reluctant to give up the old faith.

LEFT Excavating a pot set in a brick floor
ABOVE LEFT Two wooden bowling balls, probably dating to the latter part of the 16th century, were found in the pond created in the former reservoir
ABOVE Stephen Vaughan's cesspit built in the angle between the former south aisle of the church and the Lady chapel

DISCOVERY

Maps of the 1670s and 80s showed us that a street of houses, the earliest development of the suburb of Spitalfields, had formed along what was later to become Spital Square, leading out into the fields. When we came to excavate this area we discovered that this street was much older than that and that its houses were in a wonderful state of preservation.

As we removed the soil put down to raise up the ground surface in the early years of the 18th century, we could gradually make out a narrow cobbled lane. On the south side, remarkably, the north wall to the Artillery Ground still survived, despite the builders of the 1928 Spitalfields Market removing all the soil from behind it to build their basement. On the north side of the street lay a row of brick built houses, many with cellars and brick floors. One contained a niche in one wall, perhaps for holding a lamp or for keeping salt, whilst the next door house had been built by someone who had robbed the standing remains of the church for stone.

BELOW A niche in the cellar of a late 17th-century house – the niche may have been used for keeping salt or possibly for a lamp
BELOW RIGHT A row of late 17th-century houses, with a stable or barn in the centre of the row, looking back towards Stephen Vaughan's property – the lane lay to the left and the gardens to the right

The 'Principal Tenement'

Another fine building opposite Vaughan's house on the other side of the old cloister was known as the 'Principal Tenement' which, in 1580, was lived in by one Edward Isaake. The builders of this fine house reused part of the old chapel and church, and the west range of the old cloister, and built new brick walls where they were needed. The property had a yard for pulling up coaches with an entrance into the house. This entrance led into a small stone courtyard. It was surrounded on the other three sides by rooms, with that on the north side obviously being the most important, as it had a fine tiled floor. At first-floor level was a gallery, which ran all the way along the southern side of the house. This was a typical

LEFT Tiled floors and walls from the 'Principal Tenement', found in a trial trench
BELOW A painting of the frontage of Norton Folgate showing buildings whose architecture suggests a date of around 1600 or a little earlier; the building in the background immediately to the right of the tree is the 'Principal Tenement' (Guildhall Library, Corporation of London)

feature of houses of the period, where the owners and their guests could walk and admire the view or the tapestries or paintings, which their owners displayed. It was clearly a fairly grand town house of its time and its owners were obviously keen to flaunt their wealth for all to see.

West of the 'Principal Tenement' lay a complex of buildings, part stone and part half-timbered, which had formed the sisters' house, the infirmary and the latrines. These saw only minor modifications and expansion in the 16th century but were extensively remodelled in about 1600. The main building was known in the early 1700s as the 'old tavern' and next to it, at that time, was the coach house of the earls of Bolingbroke. This tavern still used some of the old medieval walls but now added new

ABOVE A brick drain, blocked with stonework presumably robbed from the former priory buildings

TOP RIGHT A small and very fine, partially gilded, wine goblet dating to the late 16th or early 17th century, discarded in an inn during the 17th century

RIGHT A detail of the copperplate map of the 1550s showing the former charnel house and pulpit centre right and the 'Principal Tenement' in the centre

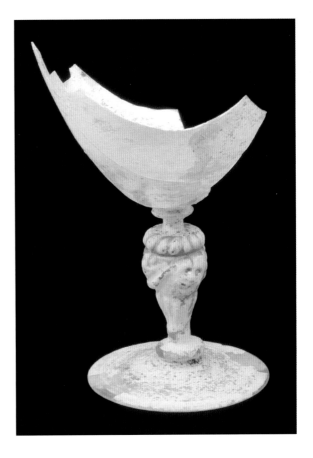

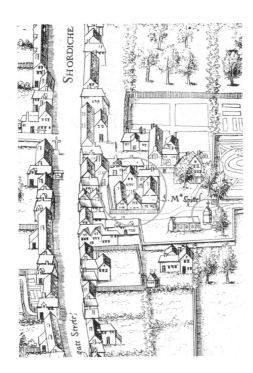

brick-built additions. A remarkable collection of late 16th- and early 17th-century glass vessels, made by Florentine glass workers in London, was recovered from the adjoining cesspit, suggesting that, at that time, it was the property of someone relatively rich. The collection contained a rare glass drinking goblet with gold leaf decoration and a unique 'trick' vessel, previously only ever seen in drawings. The trick was that there were additional spouts fed by a glass tube, which would have been obscured when the glass was full of a dark wine. When lifted to the mouth, the wine would have spilled out of the hidden spouts, covering the unwary drinker with wine.

Bolingbroke House and the earls of Bolingbroke

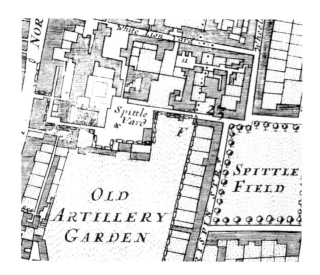

Bolingbroke House became known as such towards the end of the 17th century. Until then it was known as the 'Spittle House' and was based around a group of houses built for wealthy residents at St Mary Spital in the 14th and 15th centuries. Stephen Vaughan's grand-daughter, Elizabeth, inherited his estate after the death of her father, Sir Rowland Vaughan, in 1641. Elizabeth had married Sir Paulet St John, Second Earl of Bolingbroke, but he had already died by 1641. We do not know when the family decided to move from the old cloister buildings into a new house but we can imagine that an important family would have wanted to live in a stylish brick mansion rather than an old fashioned medieval stone building and that they decided to build themselves something that more befitted their status. It was then her son, Paulet St John, Third Earl of Bolingbroke, who rebuilt the house in about 1700. Up until then it had been a grand house in the Elizabethan style of four storeys, which faced onto Spital Yard. It was rebuilt in the new style with a courtyard at the back

TOP LEFT A detail from Morgan's map of Spitalfields from 1682 – the earl of Bolingbroke's house is that shown in elevation; the 'Spittle Field' (right) is where the original market was built

LEFT The east wall of the earls of Bolingbroke's house, overlying a medieval wall, revealed in a trial pit inside St Botolph's Hall

BELOW a group of clay pipes of the early 18th century – it is rare to find whole clay pipes as the ends were usually cut off as they became blocked

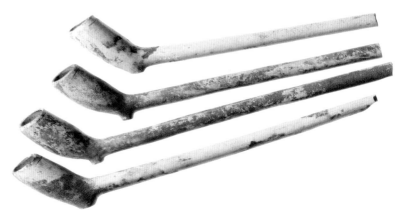

with projecting wings and a formal garden at the front, with the house reached by a grand staircase.

On Paulet St John's death in 1711, his son, Sir William St John, succeeded him and sold the house and the estate to Isaac Tillard, who was a Huguenot and was later knighted in 1722. The Tillard family continued to own the estate right up until 1919.

At the back of the ground floor of the house lay toilets over cesspits in each of the projecting wings. Contained within these were large groups of pottery and glass, discarded when the house was rebuilt; these give us a picture of the lifestyle of a member of the aristocracy in his London town house. The pottery comprised high quality tablewares, drug and ointment jars, two Chinese tea bowls and even a rare Japanese saucer with a floral decoration. The glass included bottles, cups and bowls, one of which had been gilded.

ABOVE Excavating trial pits inside St Botolph's Hall – the hall, a listed building, became the school hall of the Central Foundation School for Girls and narrowly escaped demolition in the 1970s
RIGHT A late 17th-century gilded bowl

Development of Spital Square in the 17th century

In about 1600, new houses began to appear on the Vaughan lands, east of their house. These were built alongside a narrow cobbled lane, which led out into the open fields. This lane was the forerunner of the eastern and northern arms of Spital Square, which, as we shall see later, were rebuilt in about 1700 on a much larger scale. One of the grander buildings had a semi-basement, floored in brick with two rooms, each containing a broad brick fireplace. The construction of this building entailed the demolition of parts of the Lady chapel and the removal of its foundations, and, as we shall see, many of the stones from this building were reused in another new house a little further up the street. Almost all of the new houses had their own semi-basements, often quite shallow, with drains leading out into cesspits in the back gardens. The digging of these must have disturbed bones from the cemetery beneath but this does not seem to have unduly concerned the builders or the tenants.

ABOVE A chute into a latrine in one of the late 17th-century houses – the latrine was cleared out and then floored over to extend the cellar
LEFT A brick house alongside the lane leading out to the fields

RIGHT A cesspit behind the houses, fed by a complex of brick drains – the pit was lined with horncores which were sold off after cattle had been slaughtered and often used as a cheap form of building material

One building along the lane was probably a barn or stable, whilst the rest were small brick houses. By this time, brick was the most fashionable building material but it was still relatively expensive. In order to appear fashionable, but save money at the same time, some of the walls were built from a core of stone from the demolished Lady chapel faced in brick, just as today we build in concrete faced with brick. The recovery of these stones allows us to build up a picture of the way the Lady chapel might have looked.

ABOVE The wall of one of the houses was built from the remains of the later additions to the church; the builders then faced the wall with brick to make it look fashionable

RIGHT Part of a medieval window reused in the wall

FAR RIGHT This mid 17th-century brick cellar had a double fireplace in its centre

FAR RIGHT BELOW A Delft wall tile from one of the houses

THE REDEVELOPMENT
OF SPITALFIELDS

New housing

From the latter part of the 17th century, the owners of the land in Spitalfields began to develop the area for housing, creating one of London's earliest major suburbs. London's population was growing at an unprecedented rate: in 1500 it is estimated to have reached the levels of the period before the Black Death, perhaps 80,000. By 1600 it had reached roughly 150,000 and by 1700 it had probably doubled again. This rise in population meant that the narrow streets of the old medieval walled city were too cramped to accommodate the extra numbers of people and so new suburbs were created on the edge of town. The streets leading out of the city to the outlying villages like Hackney, Shoreditch and Enfield had long been built upon, but behind them lay green fields that were ripe for development.

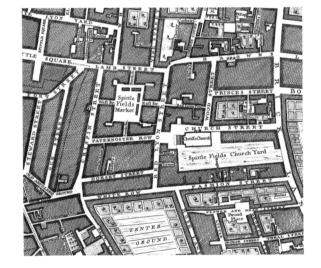

LEFT Number 1 Church Passage before construction of the market (London Metropolitan Archive)

RIGHT FROM TOP A detail from Rocque's map of 1746; two chamber pots recovered from a cesspit behind houses on Spital Square

The large rise in population was the result of a number of factors: better health and immigration both from other parts of England and from abroad. It was the groups from abroad, and one group in particular, who formed a large part of the new population in Spitalfields and this has led to Spitalfields being a focus for immigrants ever since. These were the Huguenots: French Protestants who had been granted freedom of worship by the Edict of Nantes in 1598 by the Protestant King Henry IV of France. When this edict was revoked on 22nd October 1685, Protestants who would not convert to Catholicism were given two weeks to leave the country. They became known as 'réfugies' the origin of the word refugees. They fled in droves to settle in the comparatively liberal Protestant England. Amongst other places, they moved to Canterbury and Norwich, and to Soho and Spitalfields in London.

The earliest streets to be built lay on the old fields east of the former monastery although the original Spital Square had already been formed in the 17th century. The redevelopment of the fields was started by Sir George Wheler, who owned the land and whose name is still remembered in Wheler Street. He also built a chapel for worship there, as many of the inhabitants had nowhere else to worship. The chapel was originally built from wood in 1693 but was later rebuilt in brick and eventually in 1842 became the parish church of St Mary, Spital Square, until it was closed in 1911 and then demolished.

LEFT The Wheler Chapel, later St Mary's Spital Square, on Nantes Passage (London Metropolitan Archive)

ABOVE Clearing the infilling around the late 17th-century houses in the former Artillery Ground – the walls to the left formed the cellars fronting onto Fort Street

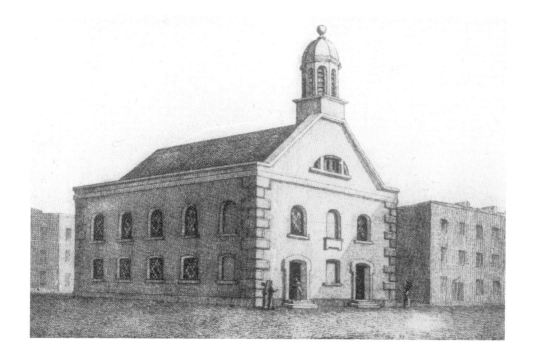

In 1682 the Artillery Ground was sold off for housing and was developed by George Bradbury and Edward Noell, who were the equivalent of speculative house builders in the later 17th century. The new streets, most of whose names echoed the former artillery practice that was held there (Fort Street, Gun Street, Artillery Passage and Artillery Lane), were lined with fine brick houses, each with its own cesspit and well in the back garden. They retained the old walls of the Artillery Ground as the back walls of the gardens and filled in the centre with new five-storey brick houses. Once the houses were built, about 1.5m of earth were dumped around them to raise up the ground surface and the lowest floor in each house was turned into a cellar. This earth was very black, full of charcoal and ash, and may have been the remains of clearance from after the Great Fire of 1666.

In about 1700 Spital Square was formed. Square is actually a bit of a misnomer, as the streets were laid out in the shape of a cross. The western arm was built in around 1700 whilst the northern and eastern were built in the 1720s and 1730s. Construction of the eastern arm involved the demolition of the original houses and the widening of the street; and when the northern arm was built, the old cloister was finally knocked down. Part of the southern side of the western arm was occupied by Bolingbroke House and part by other houses, of which the only surviving example is 37 Spital Square.

BELOW The Northumberland Head II on the corner of Gun Street and Fort Street as painted by John Crowther in 1884 (Corporation of London) BELOW RIGHT Spital Square looking east in 1909 (London Metropolitan Archive)

D I S C O V E R Y

The cellars of the old houses of Spitalfields lay directly beneath the modern streets. The houses had been demolished in the 1920s and 30s and the walls of the upper floors had literally been pushed back into the basements.

Perhaps the most poignant of our discoveries came from one of the test trenches dug in 1991. As we cleared the rubble from the cellar of a house on Fort Street we came across the concrete floor, which had been laid over the original brick floor. Along the walls were the water pipes that had served the room, which might perhaps have been used as a laundry. Against one wall was a doorway, which led out into the back garden, presumably up a short flight of steps, and in front of the doorway still lay a doormat. Close by, lying on the floor, was a jar of Boot's cream dating from the 1920s. The scene was akin to the Marie Celeste – it was almost as if the people living in the house had popped out and come back to find their house demolished. The truth is that their houses were compulsorily purchased and they merely left behind things of no value to them or things that they had forgotten. In another house we found an old iron left in a small cupboard in one of the walls.

When we came back to excavate the area fully, we found that the builders had had no scruples or moral concerns when they built the houses. Where the cesspits cut deep into the underlying medieval cemetery, one enterprising labourer decided to found the brick walls of one cesspit on the leg bones he dug up.

BELOW LEFT The cellars of houses fronting onto Steward Street
BELOW Rare fragments of late 17th-century pottery, which show strong Protestant sentiments: a depiction of the Popish Plot (above) and William and Mary who reigned together 1689–94

The inhabitants

It is only from historical records that we know that Huguenots lived in Spitalfields. The finds thrown away do not show much, if any, French influence. This tells us that the new immigrants must have left their homeland in a hurry and were content to buy and use local products. The historical records and memorials in the local churches are, however, full of French names such as Peter Douxsaint, John Lekeux and Charles De St Leu, all of whom lived in Spital Square in the 18th century. It was said that in many streets in Spitalfields it was rare to hear English spoken and the Huguenots clearly maintained some of their traditions. Tensions between them and the indigenous people led the Huguenot elders to warn that 'public feasting and dancing and games are contrary to the orderly, moderate conduct enjoined by the church, and scandalise the English nation'.

The Huguenots were famous for their weaving and that was the trade that flourished throughout Spitalfields until the 19th century. The fine houses in Spital Square were mostly the properties of the wealthy merchants who owned the businesses, whilst the surrounding streets were full of the houses of silk manufacturers, often with looms on the upper floors where the silk weavers themselves worked.

The people living in the area had an enormous variety of professions. The majority were described in the census of 1841 as either being female servants, silk manufacturers or of independent means. The next largest groups were silk weavers and labourers. Amongst others there were also carpenters, painters, porters and dressmakers, and there was even a professor of music.

RIGHT FROM TOP The front door of 32 Spital Square – the steps show how many of the ground floors of these houses were set above ground level with only semi-basements below (London Metropolitan Archive); the hall of 20 Spital Square (London Metropolitan Archive) BELOW A chamber pot containing an array of fruit pips and stones

The inhabitants of the houses on Spital Square were generally wealthier than those in the streets within the former Artillery Ground, where it is clear from census records that individuals moved house within the same street frequently. William Brandon, his wife and their daughters Caroline and Rosetta, occupied number 23 Spital Square throughout the 1830s and 1840s. William was a silk manufacturer, born in 1784, and in the census of 1851 he employed two female servants, a cook and a housemaid. His business employed 50 men and 50 women, and 40 boys and 40 girls – a very large number for the time.

Families living in Fort Street, recorded in the 1841 census, include the Goldings: Richard, a foreman born in 1792, occupied 21 Fort Street, whilst Louisa, born in 1791 occupied

number 22 and Ann a 15-year old dressmaker lived in number 23. Number 25 Fort Street was occupied by a silk manufacturer, Joseph Heylin, and his three children, William, Henry and Emma, who were all 15 at the time. Number 27 was inhabited by Walter Whitehead, a carpenter, and his wife Caroline, who were both 40, and their six children; they shared this house with a schoolmistress. Number 30 Fort St was inhabited by two different families: William Stewart (aged 65), a silk weaver and his wife Elizabeth (aged 60), with their son William and his wife Charlotte (also both weavers) and their son James; and John Ashby, a carpenter, his wife Harriet and their four young children.

The poverty of the area in the 19th and 20th centuries is made abundantly clear by the writings of those such as Jack London, who, in 1902, described the individuals sleeping on the streets outside Christchurch as:

...a welter of rags and filth, of all manner of loathsome skin diseases, open sores, bruises, grossness, indecency, leering monstrosities and bestial faces.

LEFT Brocaded silk dress woven in Spitalfields; it belonged to Anne Fanshaw, daughter of Crisp Gascoyne who became Lord Mayor of London in 1752

ABOVE RIGHT An East End London silk weaver in the late 19th century

ABOVE Detail of a panel of silk woven in Spitalfields (The Whitworth Art Gallery, The University of Manchester)

WEAVING

The weavers fell into three groups. The wealthiest were the silk merchants who might have employed many hundreds of silk weavers. Then there were the silk manufacturers, who were fairly wealthy and could often employ other weavers, sometimes with them working in the silk manufacturer's own house. Finally there were the silk weavers themselves, who were on the bottom rung of the ladder and were generally extremely poor. The poverty and poor living conditions of these people were frequent causes of riots from the 1670s for the next hundred years. Troops even had to be called in to quell the rioters. Weavers were hired, often for very short periods, and their wages were low. As the fashion for other products such as muslin grew, so the need for fine silks declined and, with it, the weaving industry.

The wealthiest merchants generally lived around Spital Square, whilst the former Old Artillery Ground area was poorer, although still with some silk manufacturers and a few merchants. The Spitalfields parish itself, outside the old monastic precincts, was generally the poorest area, inhabited by a higher proportion of weavers.

The regulation of prices by the Spitalfields Act in 1773 helped to maintain wages and conditions, and was a great improvement for many; its repeal in 1824 led to terminal decline for the industry. With the advent of the power looms in the industrial revolution, hand-woven silks became far too expensive and the industry collapsed. There were 50,000 weavers unemployed in 1832, although even as late as 1870, when the Pope wanted a seamless silk garment that had to be made by hand, Spitalfields was said to be the only place where a weaver could be found.

By the later 18th century, the French nature of the area was starting to disappear and, by the early 1800s, Jews began to live in the district. There was a strong Irish population in the area in the mid 19th century but by the end of the 19th century the area had a distinctly Jewish feel, as many thousands fled the pogroms in Eastern Europe to settle in Spitalfields and set up clothing businesses. By the latter part of the 20th century much of the Jewish nature of the area had disappeared. The Jews had moved out to be replaced by Muslims, predominantly from the Indian sub-continent and, in particular, Bangladesh.

Spitalfields seems often to have been the first port of call for poor refugees moving to London, with each group moving on once they had become established. The most obvious sign of this is the number of French churches, which became synagogues in the 19th century; one of these has now become a mosque.

Christel Church Spitalfields

Still dominating the area today, Christ Church is one of London's greatest 18th-century churches. Designed by Nicholas Hawksmoor, the church was built between 1714 and 1729 as part of a wider plan to build churches for the ever-expanding suburbs, which had no religious provision. The parish covered the area east of the old precincts of St Mary Spital. Hawksmoor was one of the great architects of his day and was also responsible for designing St George in the East and St Anne Limehouse. He was also surveyor of Westminster Abbey, designing the two towers on its west front, and he worked with Sir John Vanbrugh in designing his great 18th-century palaces at Blenheim and Castle Howard.

Almost the entire crypt has now been cleared of its burials, with many being removed without any record. However, many hundreds have been recorded and, during one phase of work, all the lead coffins were opened and the skeletons (and sometimes even mummified corpses) were recorded. These provided archaeologists with important information on the people of the area, the types of clothing they wore and the extraordinary expense many would go to in their mode of burial. A brick tomb, outside the east end of the church, contained the coffins of seven individuals including James Foot, who was 62 when he died in 1816. He was a silk manufacturer and was wealthy enough to have a memorial tablet in the church; he left £25,000 in his will, along with four houses.

The church fell into disrepair and it was proposed to demolish it in the 1960s, until local people set up a group to save the building. Various attempts have been made to repair the building, with work ongoing in 2004 finally to restore it to its former grandeur.

LEFT Christ Church
(Guildhall Library,
Corporation of London)
ABOVE Two lead coffins
inside a tomb outside
the east end of Christ
Church

Spitalfields Market

Spitalfields Market was founded on the only open section of the fields left by 1682 and, on 29 July that year, John Balch was granted a licence by Charles II to hold a market there twice a week on Thursdays and Saturdays. Ironically, Saturday is now the only day on which the market is not permitted to open. Soon the market was opened on Mondays, Wednesdays and Saturdays instead of Thursdays and Saturdays, and by the 19th century this became Tuesdays, Thursdays and Saturdays. Construction of the new market was begun in 1684 by John Metcalfe, who built four L-shaped blocks of brick houses fronting the streets around the outside, with a market building and stalls in the centre. The freehold of the site passed through various hands before the Goldsmit family sold it to the Corporation of London for £176,750 in 1902.

Originally the market sold both meat and vegetables but by the middle of the 18th century there was an intention to turn it into a fruit and vegetable market only, although the fact that many of the traders were butchers indicates that meat was still sold there. By 1803, however, it was known as a potato and fruit market, although meat was still sold there in the 1850s.

Robert Horner, formerly a porter at the market, bought the leasehold in 1875 and, after a series of legal disputes, began its rebuilding, which was ultimately to cost him £80,000. First he had the glass roof built in 1883–5 and then, after demolishing the houses surrounding the market, he had the buildings we see today constructed between 1886 and 1893. Various acts of Parliament gave the

ABOVE Excavating the cellars of Old Spitalfields Market
LEFT Fruit and vegetable traders just after the 1927 extension of the market

Borough of Stepney the right to buy the market from Horner but, eventually, the Corporation of London, who already owned the freehold, bought the leasehold and market franchise from Horner for £284,500, on 7 June 1920. The Corporation then set about the expansion of the market. The western extension to the Market was completed in 1928 and the new Fruit and Wool Exchange in 1929; the streets on the north and west side of the market were widened to give more space to traffic. The Flower Market was built on the north side of Lamb Street in 1935 and, at a similar time, Eden House was built on the corner of Spital Square for the storage of fruit.

The closure of the market and its relocation to Leyton in 1991 saw the start of the archaeological investigation of the site, which brings us back to where our story started.